SET YOURSELF FREE

*To M,
Thanks
Me — Keep pursuing
passion + congrats on
achieving your daydreams.
Best,
Mike*

SET YOURSELF FREE

DAYDREAM IT...
BELIEVE IT...
ACHIEVE IT!

MICHAEL J. LYONS

DENVER, COLORAD

Set Yourself Free
Daydream it…Believe it…Achieve it!
All Rights Reserved.
Copyright © 2017 Michael J. Lyons
v2.0

The opinions expressed in this manuscript are solely the opinions of the author and do not represent the opinions or thoughts of the publisher. The author has represented and warranted full ownership and/or legal right to publish all the materials in this book.

This book may not be reproduced, transmitted, or stored in whole or in part by any means, including graphic, electronic, or mechanical without the express written consent of the publisher except in the case of brief quotations embodied in critical articles and reviews.

Outskirts Press, Inc.
http://www.outskirtspress.com

ISBN: 978-1-4787-7020-6

Cover Photo © 2017 Michael J. Lyons. All rights reserved - used with permission.

Outskirts Press and the "OP" logo are trademarks belonging to Outskirts Press, Inc.

PRINTED IN THE UNITED STATES OF AMERICA

PRAISE FOR SET YOURSELF FREE

"*Set Yourself Free* is so good, I've had all four of my daughters read it. Michael takes his readers on a journey of introspection to reflect on what is and isn't important; what is and isn't working in their lives and what the real meaning of happiness and living life to its fullest is all about. It's a common sense book that's a quick read and full of motivating and inspiring stories and advice that every reader will benefit from."

Geoff Ballotti - President & CEO, Wyndham Hotel Group

"Everyone can find something useful in this quick-read 'gem' of a book. As a successfully retired executive, I was not sure what this book could teach me. But *Set Yourself Free* is not just another self-help book. The inspirational stories told by the author, along with Mike's simple skills-building practices, will transform your way of thinking about yourself, your career, your relationships and your life. The keys to your pursuit of happiness - no matter what your stage in life - are found in the pages of this book!!"

Elizabeth Culligan - Former President of Nabisco International and Former COO and President of A&P Supermarkets

"As a fellow Notre Dame alum, I am pleased to endorse Mike Lyons' excellent new book *Set Yourself Free*. Having overcome significant odds myself to achieve my goal of playing football for Notre Dame (and having my story immortalized on film in the movie 'Rudy'), I can easily relate to the 'Never Give Up!' attitude Mike expresses in this inspiring and insightful book. If you follow Mike's wise advice, new opportunities and successes await you."

Daniel "Rudy" Ruettiger - Motivational Speaker & Subject of the Award-Winning film "Rudy"

"In a world filled with vacuous fluff, it is nice to see an expert cut through the nonsense and establish what is real. *Set Yourself Free* is classic Lyons: fun, informative and filled with the wisdom that only a guy who has 'set himself free' could provide. In his recipe for happiness, he not only tells you HOW but more importantly WHY. The book is remarkable in its ability to 'clear the air' and reestablish those things that make the life journey everything you wanted it to be."

Steve Sullivan - Author of Wall Street Journal Best Pick "Remember This Titan" and Award-winning Performance Guru

"Michael lives the way he writes and totally walks the talk. Only someone with his life and business experience could write such an inspiring book. Out of the many golden nuggets you will find, my favorite is: 'In this day and age, we are at a critical point where those who lack self-discipline will be eaten alive by the deluge of distractions that

grow with each passing day.' I truly enjoyed it and have saved some words in my 'Quotes' notes."
Eric Rozenberg - Author of "Meeting at C- Level – An Executive Guide for Driving Strategy" and President of Swantegy

"I read the book, and I loved it. I found it to be relentlessly positive and upbeat, thoughtful and incisive, and filled with observations on life – both past and future – that I could readily identify with."
James J. Cuorato - President & CEO, Independence Visitor Center Corporation

"All the world's a stage, and I believe Mike Lyons has lived his life that way. When we initially met, we were two youngish hospitality executives making our way through the leadership of various trade associations. Upon first meeting Mike, I realized that his optimistic view of life and all around him was going to set him up with a life full of success. Also, his penchant for risk would both keep him alive in every minute and give him some stress which I never saw him demonstrate. This book captures the spirit of the young man I met so many years ago, and as the years have moved him in and out of several careers that interfaced with mine, I have always admired that indomitable spirit he displayed. His spirit lives in this book and Mike is a man who has used all of his talents to create the life he wants."
Charlotte St. Martin – President, The Broadway League Inc.

"I was so inspired by the book that I could not put it down and finished it in one reading. Michael brilliantly takes some of the great quotes of all time and weaves in his vast experiences to help readers productively streamline a 'Don't Quit - Do It' approach to inspire their lives. Entertaining … informative … engaging storytelling with concrete steps. A fantastic read!"

Deborah Gardner, CMP – Award-Winning Author, Speaker & Performance Expert

"Mike's book is filled with practical, implementable advice for anyone wanting to achieve more in their personal and professional lives. You will enjoy his conversational, honest approach that combines stories and experiences that are relatable to everyone. His advice will keep your attention and challenge you to take small steps to achieve big results."

Neen James - Attention Expert and Keynote Speaker, Neen James Inc.

"*Set Yourself Free*" will inspire you to reach new heights and enrich your life. From his life lessons learned living abroad as a young man to his experiences acting with elite Hollywood actors, Mike Lyons' first book delivers an inspirational message to anyone looking to unleash their true potential."

Edward Harris - Vice President, Marketing & Communications, Valley Forge Tourism & Convention Board

"In a world as confused, intimidating, and terrifying as ours has become, *Set Yourself Free* is an answer to prayer. In his bold, no-holds-barred words, Mike Lyons shares actual steps that bring you answers to making your life happy, and your daydreams realized no matter your age or situation. It's fascinating and hopeful. I've personally worked with and was impressed with the young man, Mike Lyons, in a theater many years ago. Today, I'm even more impressed and will use his book to enrich my life for years to come. Bravo, Mike!"
Carol Lawrence - Broadway & Television Star, Tony Award Nominee for West Side Story (Maria)

"As a seeker of wisdom on how to live my greatest purpose and vision, I have read many books on my quest. Michael Lyons' *Set Yourself Free* hits a bull's eye for me. Michael embodies resilience. Therefore the way he faced challenges in his life to live his purpose and daydreams is very inspirational, earning a place on my nightstand. As the title suggests, I recommend you set yourself free and get this book now."
Steve Sisgold, Speaker, Executive Coach, and author of "Whole Body Intelligence."

"Mike and I are about the same age, and as I read this excellent book, I began to relate many of my own personal and professional experiences to those that Mike shares and aspires others to follow. He takes us through ten steps that begin with overall happiness and closes with a needed focus on one's legacy development. This book is a must read for any individual who seeks to grow both personally and professionally, while learning how to focus on establishing goals and then achieving them."

David DuBois, CMP, CAE, CTA, FASAE - President and CEO, International Association of Exhibitions and Events

"Read this book. It's an honest and entertaining roadmap to becoming the person you know you were meant to be. Mike's personal story rings true and will make you think about your path to success. Besides being a fast and fun read, you will quickly realize that it's filled with motivational steps that you probably already knew but forgot, and need to hear again. And don't be selfish - share this book!"

Sharon Pinkenson - Executive Director, Greater Philadelphia Film Office

"Mike is living proof that most anyone can convert 'coulda, woulda, shoulda' into DONE! He also lets us know that we have many roads to travel and lots of speed bumps, but with your eye on the prize, grit, a moral compass and a deaf ear to the naysayers, anything is possible. An easy, fast read for first-time entrepreneurs or anyone who doesn't want to leave a legacy of 'coulda, woulda, shoulda.' Read it now."

Kathy Levine – Former QVC Show Host, Author of "It's Better to Laugh" and "We Should Be So Lucky."

"When it's time to re-evaluate your universe from a personal and professional perspective and live within your passion, this is your guide. Love the punch lists that will set you on the right track to embrace your moment here and now, and to help you create to maximize your life plan."
Dahlia El Gazzar – CEO, DAHLIA+ Inc. –
Brand Visionnaire + Idea Igniteur + Netweaver

"*Set Yourself Free* offers readers a host of quick inspirational advice to steer your life onto a positive course. Mike incorporates his personal life experiences with keen tips on how to reach your life goals, and it will leave you motivated to take the next steps to gain whatever you want to achieve! I highly recommend this fun, easy-to-read book to anyone who wants to change their life for the better."
Marin Bright - Founder and CEO of
Smart Meetings Media

"*Set Yourself Free* is a great read that integrates Mike's life journey with lessons learned on how to live your best life. He does a wonderful job of sharing his personal triumphs and disappointments and leads the reader to recognize life's opportunities and the relatively short time we have to act. His tips and advice for success are down to earth and grounded with experience. This book should be an assigned read for college students looking to set their career and life path, as well as business professionals seeking to be the best

they can be as they fine tune their goals and maximize their motivation to be happy and succeed!"
>   *Dan Tavrytzky - Managing Director,*
>   *DMC Network, LLC*

"Believe in yourself, and the rest will follow" – that's Mike's motto, and he certainly is proof that it works. It's your life – forget the naysayers and detractors and follow Mike's practical tips and relatable stories to daydream it, believe it and achieve your success!"
>   *Carolyn Browning, CMP, CMM – Founder &*
>   *Chief Solution Strategist, MEETing Needs*

"If you want to improve your life, read *Set Yourself Free* today. Michael Lyons delivers an honest and practical guide to being more effective, more successful and more in tune with the kind of person you are striving to become. You can finish this book in a few hours, but you will come back to it again and again as you implement Mike's many insights into your day-to-day life."
>   *Grant Snider, President & CEO,*
>   *Meeting Escrow Inc*

"What's my unfair advantage? What does 'Brand of You' mean for me? How do I pursue my happiness - and capture it? Exactly what is my legacy? Mike Lyons challenges us by asking tough, penetrating questions designed to steer us toward our best selves and away from the comfort, safety and deception of mediocrity. His breezy prose and self-deprecating style will draw you inward on a journey of self-illumination that deftly enervates our negative tendencies while releasing and elevating our deepest buried aspirations. Mike's message can indeed help to 'set yourself free' - if you'll let it."

Kevin J. Burke - Publisher/Area Director, N2 Publishing

"What I loved most about this book is how Michael shared personal triumphs and failures with us. It is not always a straight line to achieve your goals even if you give it your all. This book outlines one of my personal mantras that happiness is a choice. You are the one that decides to be happy, and only you can demonstrate the discipline to get there. No one said it would be easy, but Michael provides many tangible small steps to help us navigate this process and determine what is truly important to us both professionally and personally to live our best lives. This book is a great read at any stage of life - especially if you are ready to revisit your daydreams and take action."

Jennifer Lynn Robinson, Esquire - CEO of Purposeful Networking and President of FemCity Philadelphia

"I've known Mike Lyons for many years as the quintessential serial professional whose successful career in the hospitality industry spanned the full spectrum. Mike's gift is live communication, public speaking, serving as an MC,

facilitating, moderating and singing (he even cut a CD of Frank Sinatra favorites). In Mike's new book *Set Yourself Free* he mixes episodes from his own extraordinarily interesting life with inspiring anecdotes about others in the public eye and tells a compelling tale of courage and determination, of not letting go of your daydreams, of relentless pursuit. What makes it all so convincing and believable is that he has successfully re-invented himself and carved out a new career at age 60+. If you are unsatisfied with your life and career – this book is for you. Read it and change!"
Padraic Gilligan - Managing Partner at SoolNua, Dublin, Ireland

"Well done! Well written! Much needed! Michael's book is a perfect guide that helps one create a more effective you. Every year, sports teams reset by beginning anew during training camp. This book is your training camp to reset, rebuild, and refocus your actions to drive the results you desire and deserve. Like training camp, this book should be re-read every year to ensure that you can turn your daydreams into reality and truly 'Set Yourself Free.' Rid yourself of excuses and read this book. I am very glad I did!"
Roger Rickard, Author of 'Seven Actions of Highly Effective Advocates", and Founder of Voices in Advocacy®

"Set *Yourself Free* is easy to read with its stories of the people and situations Mike has learned from, slowly enriching his

life by making decisions that lead day by day to positive change. It also provides simple steps anyone can take and leads me to want to hear more from Mike in a face-to-face environment and to continue to be inspired by a mindset which can support the forward momentum we can all use to get a boost from time to time. Take the time – it's a fast read and so worth it!"
***Tahira Endean, CMP, DES, CED -
Event Producer, #BCTech Summit/BC
Innovation Council***

"I read *Set Yourself Free* in one sitting. It's a wonderful read, and the messages are clearly communicated, easy to follow, and every page left me looking for more. Mike's writing style resonated with me, and I enjoyed the personal stories, life experiences and lessons learned that Mike weaved into the book. *Set Yourself Free* stands out as both a positive message for self-improvement, and a simple roadmap for actually achieving more power, success and confidence in your life's journey, regardless of your personal circumstances. You'll want to keep referring to this one!"
***John Pino -- CEO, i-Meet and
Serial Entrepreneur***

"You will be inspired and motivated by *Set Yourself Free*! I have known Mike Lyons personally and professionally for many years and can attest to the many successes his life improvement prescriptions have brought to him over time.

This book is a true reflection of who he is and his wise advice will serve you well, again and again."
>   *Fritz Hoefer – President, Fast Innovations and Former Executive Vice President of Bath and Body Works*

"*Set Yourself Free* is a wonderful reminder of how we can maneuver through this crazy thing called life without losing the basic need for human engagement, the need to daydream, and to not lose our true self in the process."
>   *Michael Dominguez - Chief Sales Officer, MGM Resorts International*

"Packed with practical tips and inspirational stories, *Set Yourself Free* hits all the right notes. Mike's writing style is concise, to the point and conversational, which makes for easy reading. He invites us to push aside all the excuses and self-doubts of why we can't pursue our goals and encourages us to face our fears head-on in our pursuit of happiness. The book achieves its goal of inspiring readers to make meaningful changes in their lives."
>   *Jaki Baskow – CEO, Baskow & Associates*

DEDICATION

I dedicate this book to all the people in my life who have had a profound and powerful impact on me, in particular:

My Mom, Frances, who nurtured me throughout my adolescence and early adult life until she passed away at the young age of 54 in 1974.

My Dad, John T. Lyons Jr., who taught me that anything is possible and was my best role model and mentor.

My beautiful and steadfast wife, Lorie, who has patiently supported me and all my idiosyncrasies and entrepreneurial adventures since 1973.

My siblings Laurie, John, Elizabeth, Margaret, and Christopher who have been enthusiastic cheerleaders throughout my journey, and their life partners – affectionately known in our family as "the outlaws" – Jim Lees, Carolyn Clyde Lyons, Jim Harmon, Sam Bruno and Mari Roan Lyons.

My three amazing children—Mike, Erin, and Aimee—who have accepted and loved me with all my faults, and who have made me so proud to be their father.

My wonderful son-in-law Simon Oosthuizen and daughter-in-law Krista Foster Lyons, whom we are blessed to have in our family.

My "Sensational Seven" grandchildren—Ella, Caitlin, Jesse, Ansley, Joshua, Avery, and Logan—who inspire me, delight me, and envelop me with their unconditional love.

I owe everything I am today to all of these faithful life companions without whom life would not be worth living.

FOREWORD

As someone who grew up in poverty in the barrios of San Antonio, Texas to eventually become one of ABC-TV's first Latino correspondents, I am honored to write this foreword for my friend and fellow author Mike Lyons. Since I met Mike a few years ago, we have worked together on numerous episodes of the popular ABC-TV hidden-camera show "What Would You Do."

After getting to know Mike over the years, I see in him some of the same motivation that has pushed me throughout my life: to never settle and to keep chasing daydreams. *Set Yourself Free: Daydream it... Believe it... Achieve it!* reminds us that we all have free will to make life choices and that the best way to predict our future is to create it.

Mike spent more than 40 years juggling his day job, family commitments, and other obligations while keeping alive his desire to make a living as a full-time actor, motivational speaker, and writer. He has been relentless in his pursuit of those goals, and I admire him as someone who "walks the talk." As you read this book, you will get a peek into Mike's fierce determination to show how anyone who is focused - and visualizes his or her success - can live a better life, and create meaningful, long-lasting relationships both in the professional world and within the constellation of family and friends.

I can easily relate to many of the thought-provoking concepts and stories expressed in *Set Yourself Free*. Through my tough life experiences, I have been able to carve out a diverse and successful professional career, but more importantly, have learned valuable lessons in my personal life as well. You see, I was the kid who was never expected to amount to much.

Raised in a Spanish-speaking household, I did not learn English until I started school at the age of six. When I was 13 years old, my Dad was laid off from his job as a janitor and my family joined a caravan of migrant farmworkers and journeyed to Traverse City, Michigan to harvest cherries. Later that summer, the Quiñones family followed the migrant route to pick tomatoes outside of Toledo, Ohio. I will never forget the words my father Bruno said early one morning as we knelt on the cold, hard ground of Ohio's tomato fields: "Juanito, do you want to do this for the rest of your life? Or, do you want to get a college education?" It was a no-brainer. But, it was so much easier said than done. Whenever I would ask my teachers how I might prepare for college, they would tell me, "It's great that you have this dream of someday becoming a television reporter, but we think you should instead take classes in wood shop, metal shop, or auto mechanics." I chose to prove them wrong. Determined to overcome the Hispanic stereotype of being uneducated, I made a commitment to myself to attend college and earned a Bachelor's degree in Speech Communication from St. Mary's University in San Antonio, and a Master's degree from Columbia University's School of Journalism.

In 1982 I began my career at ABC News. During my time at ABC I have been fortunate to work on critically acclaimed news stories and specials, including in-depth reports on ABC's "20/20", "Primetime Live," Nightline and "World News Tonight." I have met and reported on people from around the world who have overcome incredible odds and seemingly impossible obstacles, rising above hardships and traumatic events to emerge as leaders and successful contributors to society.

Mike's book is an inspiring invitation to follow the examples of people who have achieved great things while casting aside negative doubts and difficult life circumstances. His insightful perspective rings true for people who are struggling to navigate their complex lives and achieve their piece of happiness.

After reading the book, I found that my life philosophy closely aligns with Mike's and the valuable information he shares in it. We both subscribe to the simple, yet brilliant, slogan coined by Nike: "Just do it!" *Set Yourself Free* will inspire you to pursue those nagging daydreams that you have swatted away with a dismissive "I can't do it" attitude. You will realize that those little voices inside your head that are telling you to "go for it" are right – not the pessimists surrounding you who constantly block your initiative with negative soundbites. If you heed Mike's advice and follow your instincts, you will achieve remarkable things. Good luck on your journey!

John Quiñones
Seven Time Emmy Award Winner
Host of ABC-TV's "What Would You Do?" &
ABC News Correspondent

TABLE OF CONTENTS

Prologue: The Early Years i

Introduction xvii

1. Happiness 1
2. Dreams versus Daydreams 15
3. The Fear Factor 21
4. Excuses, Excuses 33
5. Choices 42
6. The Procrastination Trap 46
7. Work-Life Balance 52
8. The Brand of You 61
9. Just do it! 75
10. What's Your Legacy? 82

Afterword 94

About the Author 95

Contact Information 98

PROLOGUE: THE EARLY YEARS

The viewpoints and wisdom expressed in this book are deeply rooted in my childhood. It was during the formative first twelve years of my life that my values, principles, and morals were imprinted on me. That influential period formed the foundation for the beliefs and philosophies articulated in this book, along with the powerful guidance of my parents. If one thing stands out above most in my memory bank, it was how my mother and father taught my siblings and me to live by one simple mantra: always do the right thing and respect everyone.

To "set the stage" for the content contained in *Set Yourself Free*, I am compelled to take you back to my early days to share some of my childhood memories which relate directly to the purpose of this book.

While the majority of my childhood was very happy, there were also some hard times which taught me many valuable lessons. Those experiences enabled me to weather challenges later in my life with a confidence I would not have had otherwise.

I was born and raised in suburban Philadelphia. Some of my earliest memories of attending Catholic grade school include being taught the Baltimore Catechism by stern nuns.

Question: Who made you?

Answer: God made me.

Question: Why did God make you?

Answer: To know Him and to love Him.

Preparing to spit those answers back when tested was my first introduction to intense pressure and stress (nightmares about it continue to this day!)

The turning point in my young life came in the spring of 1960. Out of the clear blue, my Dad dropped a bombshell. He announced that our family was moving to Paris, France.

My brothers, sisters, and I weren't sure how to process this news. A range of emotions swept over us—we were dumbfounded, confused, and afraid. I was nine years old, and I wasn't sure what or where France was. The playground refrain *The girls in France have ants in their pants* was the first thought that popped into my head, and that was my only reference to this faraway land where the people spoke a strange language called French.

It was a shattering development that rocked my world. Knowing we were leaving the security of our home, neighborhood, school, friends and family to go to a foreign country—where they didn't even speak English!—was a lot to wrap my head around.

After my father had told us that the experience would be terrific and that the plan was to live there for *only* four years, I ran to my room and cried myself to sleep. Four years! That's an eternity for a young lad of nine.

Dad, a charismatic and handsome man, was the oldest of eleven children from a poor South Philadelphia Irish family who grew up during the Depression. His athletic prowess as a rower on the famed Schuylkill River in Philadelphia led to his being selected as a member of the US Olympic rowing team in 1940 (though unfortunately he never competed since the games were canceled due to World War II.)

My father's good looks, intelligence, and natural networking skills helped him work his way out of his neighborhood. In early 1942 he met my beautiful mother, and after a four-month courtship, they married on the Fourth of July. Because the war was in full bloom, he was shipped off to France in the spring of 1943 to join the war effort.

While stationed in France, he fell in love with the country and Paris. In 1945 upon his return home to Philadelphia, he and my mother started a family, and he embarked on a business career. By 1960 the family had grown to six children and Dad held the important position of Advertising Director at DuPont. But my father was an epic daydreamer, and he yearned to return to the land he had discovered during his tour of duty.

Now, as an adult and father, when I look back, Dad's decision to pack up the family and move to France was very risky and half-baked at best. But at the time, he was resolute and insisted that moving to Paris was a phenomenal opportunity for the entire family and finally convinced us of this with his persuasive ways.

The whole idea of moving to Paris was instigated by a former army buddy/business colleague of my father. This man had formed a small marketing firm in Paris at the time, and he tempted my father with the opportunity to join him as a partner while painting a rosy picture filled with French francs and international adventure.

That was all my father had to hear. The attractive invitation became the impetus to round up the clan and resettle us in his romanticized French fantasy world. My devoted mother played the role of loyal "stand-by-your-man" wife and reluctantly approved the plan with appropriate apprehension due to Dad's limited and short-sighted planning.

Like some strange Alice-in-Wonderland, rabbit-hole adventure that I couldn't control, before I knew it we were driving up the New Jersey Turnpike toward New York's Idlewild Airport (now JFK Airport). A caravan of about ten vehicles filled with family and friends escorted us about halfway to New York before pulling over at a roadside gas station. Everyone got out of their cars and participated in a massive group hug with lots of tears (mainly from my aunts, who may have thought they were never going to see us again.) That moment made me even more skeptical about my father's grand plan, but there was no turning back now. We were committed. We were going to France for better or worse!

After the final farewells, we got back on the turnpike, and I looked out the back window and watched their cars grow smaller and smaller in the distance. The snapshot of my sniffling aunts still lingers in my memory. The experience was surreal, and I recall wondering if they'd still be alive when we returned from our French experiment.

The airport was crowded, noisy, and hot. The building was by far the largest edifice I had ever entered, and since this was my first airplane ride, I was completely out of sorts. The flight was delayed for a few hours due to mechanical issues, which only protracted the stress. When we finally boarded, I remember feeling very claustrophobic and nervous inside the cramped quarters of the plane.

The aircraft was a propeller-driven plane, not a jet, and the flight was very long, around eleven hours. When we finally arrived in Paris, it felt like we were on a different planet. Due to emotional and physical exhaustion and the strange sensation of jet lag, we were like little zombies. The authorities herded us through a long customs line. I recall my Dad, who knew about ten words of French—another miscalculation when he decided to take us to a foreign country—trying to communicate and explain to the French customs agent that the eight of us were a family. The agent was a no-nonsense, unfriendly chap who was agitated and spoke rapidly (which none of us could understand, of course.) *Man, this isn't the picture Daddy painted. What's next?* I thought.

Eventually, we passed through customs, and once out of the airport, we faced our second challenge: cramming all eight of us into two tiny taxis, along with all of our luggage. Complicating matters, the taxi drivers did not speak English (no surprise there.) A comical episode ensued as my father and the taxi drivers attempted to communicate through the drivers' broken English and my father's ten words of French, supplemented by a strange animated sign language he invented on the spot.

After reaching our destination, an argument unfolded as my father accused the drivers of overcharging us by taking a circuitous route. (Keep in mind that dear old Dad hadn't been to Paris since 1945 and probably had no clue about the city's geography.) He was convinced that he was being ripped off, and after a lot of cursing and shouting, they agreed to a number even though neither side appeared satisfied with the outcome.

At least we were finally at our new "home." After what seemed like an eternity getting there through jet lag, food deprivation, dehydration, and emotional distress - we were ready to collapse. But even at that young age, and in my discombobulated state, I noticed immediately that our new home wasn't a house like we were accustomed to back in the good old USA. Instead, it was a tiny one-bedroom flat with a teensy-weensy bathroom (with little to no water pressure or hot water) – and certainly not designed for eight people!

Dad had asked his bachelor business partner to arrange our accommodations, and that is what he came up with. Mom's stand-by-your-man demeanor disintegrated before our eyes. As the kids foraged for food in the small cubicle generously described as the kitchen, Mom and Dad had their first official argument on French soil. Mom won, and Dad's immediate priority was to find more suitable housing.

Meanwhile, we scavengers came up with scant options in the food department (the moldy Camembert cheese was not very appealing.) Dad reached into his pocket, pulled out a ten centimes coin (about a nickel), and told my older brother John and me to walk down the street to the *boulangerie* (bakery) to buy a baguette. "A what?" we asked.

"A baguette," he growled back, clearly showing the stress of his quarrel with Mom. "Go to the store and say 'Je suis Americain, une baguette'. It means I am American, one loaf of bread" he said. We agreed immediately to get away from the tension and take advantage of an opportunity to explore our new surroundings.

As we walked to the store I kept repeating over and over "Je suis Americain, une baguette." I was petrified that when we got there, I wouldn't remember it, and I sure as heck was not going back without accomplishing our mission.

When we arrived at the boulangerie, the smell of the baked goods was the best scent I had ever encountered in my life. Wow, what a place! John and I just stood there taking it all in—row after row of freshly baked baguettes, croissants, and other French pastries. The mouthwatering aroma was overwhelming, and we stood there silently, drawn into the whole scene.

Finally, a portly woman behind the counter greeted us with "Bonjour, qu'est-ce-que vous voulez?" (Hello, what do you want?) Her rapid tongue jolted us out of our stupor and back to reality, but by then I had forgotten the magic phrase. I stuttered and stumbled and looked at John for help, but he couldn't remember the phrase either. So we spoke in English, but she couldn't understand us. We frantically pointed at all the bread but there were too many types, and we weren't sure which one was the … the … the baguette. Yes, that's it! A baguette! Suddenly I blurted out, "Je suis Americain, une baguette."

The woman bellowed with laughter and answered back, "Oh, vous êtes Americains." She let out another chuckle, waddled over to the rack, grabbed a warm baguette, wrapped it in tissue, and handed it to us. I gave her the coin, and she gave me change. For some reason (probably because of the taxi fare disagreement), the thought occurred to me that she hadn't given us the right amount of change back. So I gave her the old stink eye, turned on my heels, and walked out with my bodyguard brother right behind me.

Success! We had negotiated our first business transaction in our new country, though I still felt like we had been hoodwinked. As we were walking home, the bread was too irresistible, so John and I began to break off little chunks and devoured them. It was the best bread we had ever tasted. The more we ate, the more we wanted. It was like a drug—we couldn't stop. We knew full well that we were going to be in big trouble bringing home a half-eaten loaf, but we didn't care. Whatever the punishment, the delicious bread was worth it.

By the time we got back to our palatial quarters, about a third of the baguette was left. My father, who was apparently still stressed from the fight with Mom, scolded us and made us go back to the store to buy another loaf, which we gladly did.

We lived in the flat for about six weeks until Dad found another place. The cramped quarters tested everyone's patience and tempers often flared. Clothes, sleeping bags, and household items were strewn everywhere. There wasn't much to do since there was no TV, so our parents encouraged us to play outside in the park across the street. Essentially, we were bored prisoners who lived in a tiny cell awaiting the day of our release.

The new house Dad found was located in the suburbs of Paris. It was a fully furnished rental home, and the owners were temporarily living in Italy. It was a lovely place with plenty of room, and the new location changed our moods dramatically.

A few weeks after we moved in, the new school year began. Our parents decided to enroll us in French schools even though none of us could speak a word of French (other than my infamous bread sentence.) I had never heard the phrase "sink or swim" before, but that was what my Dad responded when we asked him how we were going to understand the teacher and our fellow students. We all felt like lambs being led to slaughter who had no choice or say in the matter.

I will never forget the first day of school. My father had imported his car from the US, so he wouldn't have to buy one in France. The car was a huge gas-guzzling Lincoln Continental which dwarfed the small French cars and didn't quite fit on the narrow streets of Paris. Not a good idea to bring it over, particularly because of the exorbitant fuel prices. But it was a very cool automobile with electric windows and leather seats and looked like it belonged in a presidential motorcade.

As we pulled up to the school, the French schoolboys ran alongside it, shouting and waving at me in the back seat like I was a rock star. When I got out of the car, I felt like a celebrity and the novelty of being an American gave me instant star status.

Inside the classroom was a different story. My frustrated teacher knew a few English words, but not enough to communicate to me what she was saying. For the first semester, I sat in the back of the room and listened as intently as I could, trying to pick up the gist of what she was saying.

At the end of the first semester, I ranked last in the class. Then an amazing thing happened: I started to pick up the language through interaction with my French classmates. At the end of the school year, my command of French qualified me for advancement to the next grade (just barely.) And out on the playground, I began to develop soccer skills and started to bond with my new friends.

While my school life was going well, things on the home front were not. The business that my father and his partner had formed ended badly, leaving him out of work and deep in debt. Compounding the situation, my mother was dealing with some ongoing health issues that forced her to spend most of her time in bed. My eighteen-year-old sister Laurie took on the household duties, while my father attempted to find work.

In spite of my parents' best efforts to camouflage the seriousness of our situation, we all knew the severity of it. I felt sad, helpless, and hopeless during this period until things eventually started to turn around. Doctors at the American Hospital of Paris prescribed a new drug for Mom (cortisone), which got her back on her feet. My father finally found work at an American advertising agency's Paris office, and badly needed income flowed back into the household.

From that point on, our time in France was punctuated with wonderful family memories: picnics in the famous

Bois de Boulogne Park, visits to museums and chateaux, and a summer vacation with my French classmates on the coast of France, among other memorable times.

One day, a life-changing event occurred. My father came home from work and announced that he was going to take me to audition the following day for an American commercial they were shooting in Paris. They needed a kid who looked American, and it just so happened that I had reddish hair and freckles—a vague resemblance to Ron Howard who was starring as Opie in *The Andy Griffith Show* at that time. Even though I didn't have a clue about what an audition was or how the process worked, I was happy to give it a shot. It sounded like fun.

The commercial was for the pasta company Buitoni, and the next day at the audition, I was selected! The commercial was shot the following week, and suddenly I was a professional actor. Voilà!

Dad hired a talent agent, and I began to book jobs on a sporadic basis, primarily commercials and dubbing work for movies in both French and English (By then I spoke fluent French with no hint of an American accent.)

The highlight of my young acting career came in September 1962 when they were filming the movie *Paris When It Sizzles*. The film starred three Hollywood legends: Audrey Hepburn, William Holden, and Tony Curtis. My part was small, but I exchanged dialogue with Tony Curtis in a scene shot at night at the base of the Eiffel Tower. Tony was friendly and playful, and it was fun rehearsing lines with him.

The thing I remember most about Tony was him constantly lighting up cigarette after cigarette. He'd take a few puffs, stomp on it, and then light up another. When we were done, I looked at the ground, and there were at least a dozen cigarettes laying there, all half-smoked.

Being on the set of a major motion picture was pretty heady stuff for an eleven-year-old, but as much as my father tried to explain the significance of it to me, I didn't get it. I vividly recall the beautiful, elegant and gracious Audrey Hepburn walking up to me and striking up a conversation during a break in the filming. She was sweet and genuinely interested in learning more about me and my background. I treasure that conversation now, though at the time I just thought she was a nice lady.

My childhood acting experiences in France lit a flame that led to my desire to pursue acting as a career and formed the foundation for the next chapter of my life.

In 1963, when I was twelve, my family and I returned home to Philadelphia. Coming back to the US was a very strange sensation for my siblings and me. It was as if we had been in a time bubble for three years. Reintegrating into American culture, new schools, and a new home took some time.

Shortly after we returned to the US, President John F. Kennedy was assassinated. His slaying, along with other tumultuous events of the 60s—the deaths of Martin Luther King and Robert F. Kennedy, civil rights unrest, the 1968 riots at the Chicago Democratic Convention, and the nagging US involvement in Vietnam—made for an eye-opening transition into adolescence and collegiate life.

Today, I point back to those early years in France as a major influence in my life, including planting the seed that led to my current career as an actor, writer, and professional speaker fifty-six years later!

INTRODUCTION

This book will challenge you to look inward and reflect on your life and career goals, and assess where they stand relative to the items on your bucket list. And if you don't have a bucket list, perhaps it's time to write one. After reading this book, you will walk away with tangible, manageable tips that can be implemented immediately to keep you on track to follow through on your daydreams.

Set Yourself Free: Daydream it… Believe it… Achieve it! is the culmination of a lifetime of experiences that began when I was bitten by the acting bug in France at the age of ten. From that point on I set my sights on becoming an actor. Even at that young age, I instinctively knew that acting was my calling. As the years went by, I pointed myself towards a career in the performing arts and honed my craft in numerous theatrical plays throughout high school and college.

But the goal of an acting career was eventually sidetracked by the realities of life and my personal choices: I chose to marry young, and I chose the business world instead of an acting career. Why?—because I fell prey to fear and insecurities and dwelled on the uncertainty and inherent risks of an acting career, instead of focusing on being successful.

At the time, I was too young and ignorant to realize that risk is worth taking if you believe in yourself. So I abandoned the actor career path and tended to the needs of my growing family, plugging along at work even though my business career left a void in my life.

But as we all know, life has a way of taking unexpected turns that change our destiny. Twenty-seven years ago when I realized that five years from then all three of my children would be in college at the same time and that I had nothing saved, I came up with a solution: become an actor in TV commercials while keeping my day job in the business world. I knew that commercials paid handsome residuals (each time a commercial is shown on TV, the actor earns royalties), and if I could make just a few spots, the college fund would grow quickly. The plan sounded easy to me in my overly confident state. I mean, how hard could it be?

At that time I was working in New York City, and I knew that many commercials were cast and shot there. All I had to do was find a talent agent who would represent me and submit me for auditions and casting calls.

I was ridiculously naïve, of course. I quickly learned what thousands of other aspiring actors already knew:

Commercial acting is a highly competitive business with tons of talented professionals competing for a small number of roles. In fact, many seasoned professionals with years of experience never land a nationally broadcasted commercial.

After about a year of having doors closed in my face and getting hundreds of "No, thank you" responses to my letters and phone calls (and just before I was about to give up), an agent took a chance on me and started sending me on auditions. Within two months, I landed a commercial for Honey Bunches of Oats cereal. From there I joined Screen Actors Guild (SAG) and began to book more commercials, some TV roles, and other acting jobs on a regular basis including *All My Children* and an Advil spot that ran on national television for four years.

The income derived from my acting jobs during that period paid for all three of my kids' college education expenses with a few dollars to spare.

So the plan worked! I was able to keep my regular job, earn substantial extra money through my sideline career as an actor, and as a bonus, carve out a little happiness working on acting projects that satisfied my cravings for the career I had consciously, though regrettably, left behind at age twenty-one.

As the years went by, I maintained both careers and worked sporadically on a variety of acting projects including the film *The Sixth Sense* and the popular HBO series *Veep*, among others. I was also fortunate to land a steady gig (in my spare time) as a Product Host on the home shopping network QVC. That ride lasted ten years, and I accumulated more than 350 live appearances.

Around that time, I was tempted to jump full-time into acting, but family responsibilities and fear kept me from taking the leap. Getting a paycheck every two weeks creates a sense of security and complacency, and the thought of going weeks or months without an acting job, quite frankly, scared me (and my wife!)

In 2014, at the age of sixty-three, the tug of the acting daydream (as well as my desire to grow my fledgling career as a professional speaker), became so strong that I took the plunge into the deep end of the pool. With my wonderful wife's full support I quit my secure, high-paying day job with no guarantees other than a belief in myself and confidence that I would succeed—regardless of the perceived and real obstacles.

When that decision was made, I opened the door to living the rest of my life doing the things I am passionate about. Foolish? Perhaps, but I knew I wouldn't go to my grave wondering *What if?*

I wrote this book to pass on what I have learned and to encourage people to pursue *their* daydreams. It took me a long time to realize that anyone can achieve what he or she daydreams about if they are willing to make the commitment.

Achieving difficult goals has been accomplished millions of times throughout history. People overcome odds, climb mountains, break sports records, and do what is seemingly impossible. Many start businesses, some of which fail, then start others until they find the right formula. Walt Disney and Thomas Edison are classic examples.

Throughout our lives, we have heard over and over that if we can visualize where we want to be and follow the path to get there, success can be ours. And yet, for some reason we are suspicious, skeptical, or paralyzed with fear. No one said it would be easy, or without obstacles and setbacks (in fact, you can count on them), but you only get one life, and our time here is relatively short —so why not go for it?!

This is particularly true in our wildly unpredictable world. Since 9/11, numerous world events, catastrophes, and unforeseen occurrences have given us the incentive to pause and re-evaluate our futures and to cherish each moment we have been given. In the past decade, we have weathered the worst recession since the Great Depression – which saw many people lose their jobs or have them downsized.

Meanwhile, the world has become an increasingly complex place where random acts of terrorism and other violence pop up regularly across the globe, altering the lives of people in an instant. With this ever-changing world and uncertain times as a backdrop, it's an ideal time to take stock of where we've been, where we are, and most importantly, where we want to go. And perhaps the timing for a change in life path is now.

I feel qualified to walk with you on this journey. My credentials include a rich and diverse career in multiple industries and job roles, and extensive travel around the US and the world, all of which has shaped my perspective and enhanced my experience in a variety of different ways. Altogether, I have worked for twelve different companies, including two start-ups, plus four other entrepreneurial businesses I started on my own on the side—all with varying degrees of risk, success, and failure. Also, my experiences as a professional actor, speaker, consultant, and writer have expanded my view of the world and introduced me to many interesting characters, both real and fictional.

As you will see, I am a serial risk-taker who enjoys the thrill of trying new things (without fear of failure.) I hope that some of my adventurous risk-taking mindset will rub off on you as you read this book. I firmly believe that we all can (and must) conquer the internal *No* voice that holds us back from accomplishing the things we hope to achieve. So read on with an open mind, and **Set Yourself Free!**

Chapter 1

HAPPINESS

> "The Constitution only guarantees people the right to pursue happiness. You have to catch it yourself."
>
> —*Benjamin Franklin*

We are all familiar with the famous phrase *pursuit of happiness* contained in one of our nation's most precious documents, the Declaration of Independence. In that text, our forefathers recognize that:

> All men are created equal, that they are endowed by their Creator with certain unalienable rights that among these are life, liberty and the pursuit of happiness.

Accordingly, we consider these rights to be sacred, and we strive to achieve them.

We all want to enjoy a full life with deep emotional connections with people we love, find satisfaction in what we do each day for a living, and live comfortably with adequate food, shelter, and clothing. But in the 241 years since those words were written, our complex and ever-changing world have made it more challenging to find that magic bullet. There is no one-size-fits-all path to happiness, and a lot of *stuff* gets in the way of getting there. An individual's pursuit of happiness can be thwarted by many different factors: bad habits, guilt, fuzzy expectations, health issues, unhealthy relationships, financial trials, and so on. Finding the right formula for happiness is challenging because each person is uniquely different.

Throughout history, philosophers and famous personalities have coined their definitions of happiness. Here is one of my favorites:

> "The person born with a talent they are meant to use will find their greatest happiness in using it."
> —*Johann Wolfgang von Goethe*

Goethe's quote restates a theme that is threaded throughout this book. Every person has a talent, and if it is used, a person's path to happiness becomes shorter and clearer.

Many people spend their whole lives working in jobs that do not suit their natural skills or talents— either in

HAPPINESS

occupations they were forced into because of parental pressure, the family business, college majors chosen blindly, or chance.

Where are you right now in your life and career? Do you ever think about it? Do you spend a lot of time complaining about your relationships, the type of work you do, where you live, who your friends are, *etc.*, but do absolutely nothing to change the situation?

Are you too tired or lazy to change? Do you feel trapped by your responsibilities with no apparent solution? Do you blame other people for your problems, or look in the mirror and hold yourself accountable for your actions?

Do you feel limited regarding available resources or opportunities and think *I'll just wait it out… Things are bound to get better eventually.* Really? If you truly think that, you are living a fairytale. Guess what? You are the only one who can redirect the course of your life and the only way to redirect your life is to take action.

With these important questions, there are choices. You can either choose to ignore them and remain dissatisfied, or you can do something about it. The principles in this book address the lack of satisfaction with a person's personal life, professional life, or both.

When examining where you are, it is helpful to ask yourself how you arrived at your current situation. Can you identify turning points that pushed you away from where you want to be? In some cases, our life circumstances steered us to a place we had little or no control over – other factors such as our DNA; where we grew up; our education (or lack thereof); the influence of our parents, siblings, and friends; and our financial status all played a role. Were there circumstances beyond your control that impacted where you are today? Well, the good news is that it's never too late to make a change.

Depending on whose survey results you believe in, roughly two-thirds of the people queried (in multiple studies) responded that they are not 100% happy with the way their lives were progressing. Whether those figures reflect their personal life, career, or both, the fact is the majority of the population are, at this very moment, dissatisfied. And frustrated. And, in most cases, unsure about how to get out of their vicious cycle.

Most people can quickly conjure up excuses why they are powerless to change, such as "I'm too old," "I'm too poor," "I'm too depressed," "I'm too inexperienced," *etc*. But the fact is other people have overcome all of those situations (and much worse) and have climbed out of their ruts to become happy, successful, fulfilled individuals.

HAPPINESS

Every one of us is blessed with unique abilities and skills. For some individuals these talents are self-evident; for others, it requires looking deep within themselves. The process of identifying a person's talents varies from person to person. There is no set timetable. Determining your sense of self is a gradual, lifelong undertaking. Sometimes we discover our true calling early in life, sometimes in the middle, and other times near the end. If not immediately evident, your true talents will eventually emerge and will lead you to a crossroad of choices that will ultimately determine your sense of self.

When you arrive at that point, you can choose to make a change or stay the course. If you make the choice to change, it is then about identifying the actions required that will be stepping stones to true happiness in the long run, rather than choosing actions that are bound to bring disappointment and despair.

Part of the challenge is that we have a lifetime of bad habits to change. On the one hand, we have a hyperactive mind to pacify; on the other, a dull mind that needs to wake up. Happiness requires discipline and effort. But nourished by happiness, discipline becomes joyful, and effort becomes easier and more relaxed. Happiness is truly a self-fulfilling prophecy if you feed it properly, and are consistent in your actions and mindset.

SET YOURSELF FREE

Here are five key happiness concepts:

1. You deserve to be happy.

> "Carpe diem! Rejoice while you are alive;
> enjoy the day; live life to the fullest;
> make the most of what you have. It is
> later than you think."
> —*Horace*

Happiness is a birthright and challenges are temporary setbacks. Happiness is a natural state for human beings, so embrace this thought and go with it.

2. Take personal responsibility for your life choices.

> "There are two primary choices in life: to
> accept conditions as they exist, or accept
> the responsibility for changing them."
> —*Denis Waitley*

Happiness is a choice. Everyone can choose to be happy and choose to increase their happiness level. Stop blaming others for choices you've made in your life, and don't waste energy portraying yourself as a victim. Take personal responsibility for everything you do, and begin to trust yourself to choose those things that will ultimately lead to your happiness. When you stop blaming others and take responsibility for all the decisions in your life, you truly set yourself free so you can embark on the true path towards happiness.

3. Increase your social connections.

> "You can make more friends in two months by becoming interested in other people than you can in two years by trying to get other people interested in you."
>
> —*Dale Carnegie*

As Dale Carnegie implies, putting other people first, ahead of your interests, pays dividends *Vis* à *Vis* increasing your social connections. And studies have shown that people who have close personal connections with others feel happier about themselves. Isn't it true that when you focus your efforts on making other people feel good about themselves, you feel better about yourself, and develop a deeper sense of satisfaction and happiness?

Which do you enjoy more: giving a gift or receiving one? As a child, I nearly burst with anticipation when my parents opened my modest Christmas gift and card. Their reactions provided immediate positive feedback.

The joy of giving does not wane as we grow older. So reach out, make more connections, and be of service to others. You will be rewarded many times over.

Next, surround yourself with people who are positive influences in your life. Eliminate (or at least limit) the number of negative people you associate with every day. Negative people spread cancer that afflicts everyone around them. They suck the life and happiness right out of you. Rather, spend time with people who build you up or see the good in you.

My Dad used to call me "Champion" or "My Golden Son." After years of hearing those terms consistently, my confidence and ego were bolstered, and it fueled my belief that I could achieve difficult goals which, on the surface, appeared unreachable.

4. Don't compare yourself to others.

> "Be a first-rate version of yourself, not a second-rate version of someone else."
>
> —Judy Garland

When I was a teenager, I followed in my older brother John's footsteps. Whatever he did, I pursued as well. We both worked at the same country club during high school, attended the University of Notre Dame, and were fencers on the college team. After graduation, I went to work for the same company where he was employed. Even though he was an excellent role model and mentor, it wasn't healthy that I intentionally replicated his every move all the time.

HAPPINESS

I remember trying to talk and act like him 24/7, but deep down I knew I could never be him, or – harder for me to accept – *be liked* as much as he was. (John is quite charismatic.) It was difficult for me to face the fact that I would never measure up to his standards. I finally realized that I had to be *me*, not a facsimile of him. And once I focused on that, I felt a burden lifted, and started to live my life in earnest.

Though it may be hard not to compare ourselves with others, it's best to resist that temptation. There will always be someone else who seems to have more than you and appears to be happier. But appearances can be deceiving, as we know. The adage "Money can't buy happiness" has stood the test of time.

Our culture idolizes celebrities, and we sometimes wish we could exchange lives with them – after all, they are rich, famous, and give the impression that they have it all. But we also read on a regular basis about the problems and issues they have: divorce(s), drug addiction, short-lived success, to name but a few. Many, if not most, struggle just like us "regular folks" do with our quest for happiness. All too often, celebrities die young because of their careless actions – usually, and tragically, because of drugs that they took to help them escape from their unhappy realities.

When you stop comparing yourself to others and just live your life, your happiness and chances of life satisfaction will increase. You come to the realization like I did that being the best *you* is good enough, or even better!

5. Expect good things to happen to you.

> "The foolish man seeks happiness in the distance; the wise man grows it under his feet."
>
> —*James Oppenheim*

Happy people tend to be optimists. When we expect good things to happen in our lives, they usually do. They happen because we are in a positive state of mindful expectation, and because an optimistic outlook governs and guides our actions. When we feel hopeful about our lives and the people in them, it generates a sense of well-being. Conversely, if we walk around with a scowl on our face all day long, or act grumpy – while all the time pushing people away – that has a direct impact on our degree of happiness.

Happy people want to be around other happy people. Most people are inherently good, and life is a miraculous gift, so seeking out positive people, experiences, and environments will inevitably amp up your level of happiness.

Moreover, expecting good things to happen becomes self-fulfilling. In other words, the more you expect pleasant things to happen, the more they *will* happen, thereby increasing your chances of leading a happier, more fulfilled life.

In my research, I found another interesting nugget on this subject. According to psychologist Martin Seligman, author of *Authentic Happiness*, happiness relates to how we live our life in relation to what we have, rather than an accumulation of perceived "good things" like wealth, good looks, a terrific job or social status.

Seligman found that contentment does not result from a perfect job, a perfect family, or a perfect society. Rather, happiness is a combination of many things. It is also a result of trying your best to make the most of what you were born with or have developed over time, and putting your talents to good use in the service of others.

The happiest people in the world are not those who have perfect lives, but rather those who have learned to live an "imperfect" life, in spite of their situation.

I saw this first-hand in Africa many years ago when my wife and I visited our youngest daughter Aimee who was serving in the Peace Corps at the time. Aimee lived for two years in a small remote village in the West African nation of Togo. There was no running water or electricity, a very limited food supply and virtually no health care.

When we arrived, the residents greeted us warmly with hugs, smiles, and laughter, and organized a welcome celebration with music, dancing, and food, which made us feel very special. Most of the villagers attended, and it was such a joy to see everyone happy and having a great time.

In spite of their meager resources, we could see that they lived in harmony and peace, and respected each other. What was also evident to us was how everyone in the village helped and supported others in time of need. They shared food, took turns around the clock caring for the sick, and children were happy and carefree because they were raised lovingly in a safe environment with the entire village watching over them.

That African experience put happiness in perspective for us, and when day-to-day trivial things go wrong, I try to remember that they are nothing but "first-world problems" as Aimee likes to say.

One of the other things I took away from that visit to Togo was how everyone was smiling all the time. It makes you realize the power of a smile as a contributor to your daily happiness quota. A simple smile can turn a difficult situation into a positive one in a second. Frequently when I am out in public I conduct an informal experiment: I find that whenever I smile at someone, they invariably smile back. Smiling is a natural reflex.

HAPPINESS

For example, if you are driving in heavy traffic where everyone is on a high "road rage" alert, and you want to swing into the next lane – simply signal politely to the car next to you while flashing a sincere smile, and chances are they'll let you in. So much better than having them point their middle finger at you because you tried to force your way into their lane without any communication or eye contact.

Years ago, two phrases popped into my head when I was thinking about this: "A smile is your best friend" and "A smile changes everything." When I utter these expressions, my children snicker and call these sayings corny. But I like them and stand by them because I believe a genuine smile used often is like a drug that delivers steady doses of happiness.

Cultivating a habit of happiness is an ongoing process that requires attention, commitment and the ability to distinguish between "perishable" and "durable" items of happiness. Attempting to seize happiness on demand involves perishable items like drugs, food, clothes, and sex. Perishable items only provide momentary pleasure, not long-term happiness. Durable items, on the other hand, bring about an ongoing, prolonged state of happiness. Acts of kindness are a good example of durable items of happiness, similar to making deposits into a happiness savings account.

We also have to remember that in our imperfect world, there are many barriers to happiness. Few people on the planet possess perfect jobs, sufficient wealth, excellent health and strong relationships with all the people in their lives, all at the same time. Everyone has challenges and hurdles in their quest for happiness, but contentment will usually follow when you live your life consistent with your values and what you have, rather than wanting or regretting what you don't have.

Try to approach each day with an "always-good" attitude. When we respond to the oft-asked question "How are you?" most people routinely respond with "Good or fine." When people ask me that question, my response is "Always good" — I say it because I believe it. Regardless of what kind of day I may be having, saying that phrase out loud positively influences my mindset and attitude. And what's interesting is that many people will respond with "I like that," or "I need to adopt that."

Chapter 2

DREAMS VERSUS DAYDREAMS

"Everything starts as somebody's daydream."

—*Larry Niven*

Dream
Noun, often attributive \'drēm\
: a series of thoughts, visions, or feelings that happen during sleep

Daydream
Noun \'dā-ˌdrēm\
: pleasant thoughts about your life or future that you have while you are awake

We hear and talk about dreams all the time: the house of our dreams, the car of our dreams, our dream job, *etc*. But do we *dream* about those things? Usually not. Because, as the dictionary definition above implies, we don't have control over *what* we dream about. When we go to sleep, we don't normally say "Tonight I think I'll dream about my perfect vacation." We don't because we are powerless about what our dreams will be. For me, they're usually a strange mish-mash of events and people with no clear connection (especially if I had Chinese food for dinner before going to bed!)

In my opinion, the word "dream" has been misused in advertising, movies, sports stories and other media references. In many instances, it should be replaced by the more fitting word daydream.

Daydreams are "pleasant thoughts about your life or future that you have while you are awake." And we all daydream … a lot. Throughout the course of the day we find ourselves daydreaming in various situations: while we're driving; sitting in a boring meeting; disengaged in a conversation we are having, or in church pretending to listen to a dull sermon.

When we daydream, we drift off mentally to some happy place where we fantasize about things we'd rather be doing. Or jobs we covet. Or relationships we'd prefer over the ones we currently have, or any number of things that, for the moment, make us feel good (like winning the lottery!) Then BAM! We snap back to reality. The boss in your meeting says "Well, what do you think about that idea?" Or your spouse sitting next to you in the car asks "What are you thinking about?" Or the sermon is finally

DREAMS VERSUS DAYDREAMS

over, and it's time to kneel (and you have no clue what the pastor just said for the last 20 minutes.)

The perfect home, the fancy car, that great family vacation, the promotion at work, starting a new business ... that's what we daydream about. And yet, in most cases, once we come out of our trance, we pick up where we left off and forget about the things we just daydreamed about. Oh, we might write a note to ourselves like "Look into starting a dance studio," or "Write a book," or "Go back into teaching;" but in most cases, that's where it stops.

So how do successful and happy people translate their daydreams into reality? *They focus on the prize.*

When you speak to world-class athletes and Olympic champions and ask them what motivates them, they consistently talk about how they "visualize." They picture what it will feel like when the gold medal is placed around their neck, or when they hoist the championship trophy over their head. They can *see* it in their mind! And they stay laser-focused on that vision through years of sweat, practice, and setbacks until they reach their goal.

Once you've tasted success and achieve a milestone, it becomes easier because you gain confidence and want to re-experience that euphoric feeling of having reached that objective. You naturally begin to imagine more and more possibilities, and feed off of the adrenaline high that comes with having experienced that sense of accomplishment. But until you get there, your daydreams serve as motivation to keep you focused, while using the visualization technique along the way.

For example, if you want to start a restaurant, begin by picturing every detail in your head (and then on paper): the layout, décor, menu, kitchen set-up, staff, *etc*. Share that vision with people who you know will support you and be your cheerleaders throughout the process. Be sure to stay away from naysayers. They're the ones who will give you all the reasons why your restaurant will fail.

Case in point: Years ago when I decided to do TV commercials to help pay for my kids' college educations, my first task was getting headshots (photos) taken. When the proofs came back, I wanted to get some feedback from friends and family members I trusted so they could weigh in on which shots they thought were the best.

I was surprised when I heard comments like "You'll never be able to do commercials…There's too much competition…You don't know anything about it… Do you really think you can act?" I was taken aback that some people who I assumed would be supporters turned out to be detractors. And yet, in a sense, I am thankful that they reacted that way because it motivated me, even more, to prove them wrong.

DREAMS VERSUS DAYDREAMS

The path is not always an easy one to follow. It's difficult to maintain motivation over time, even for the most optimistic person. Other distractions and negative thoughts start to creep into your head, challenging your commitment to the goal.

I vividly recall, all those years ago, walking down the street on a rainy day in New York City after yet another rejection from a casting director, thinking to myself "This will never work…They were right… I can't do this." But then I recalled a Chinese proverb I had heard years earlier:

> *The temptation to quit will be greatest just before you are about to succeed.*

And that thought propelled me to move forward and not give up.

Shortly after that, I landed my first national television commercial, which was the beginning of a long run that eventually helped me reach my goal of paying for my children's college educations solely through my acting income.

So keep your end-goal vision in front of you, and use it as the impetus to drive your actions. Every time your imagination starts to stir with new ideas, write them down and get excited about plotting the next steps towards your version of the gold-medal platform.

SET YOURSELF FREE

It's also important to remember that sometimes you might fall short of your ultimate goal on the first try, but were quite successful nonetheless in reaching a milestone on your journey. Don't stop, or settle if you don't cross the finish line. In the Olympics example, winning a silver or a bronze medal is certainly nothing to be ashamed of. There are countless athletes who didn't win gold on their first try but came back four years later and claimed the prize. It's the same for us. Perhaps on our first attempt, we didn't accomplish what we set out to do, but that experience should be used as a stepping stone to keep working towards achieving the goal.

Chapter 3

THE FEAR FACTOR

> "The only thing we have
> to fear is fear itself."
>
> —*Franklin D. Roosevelt*

And so we daydream and fantasize and think happy thoughts until we snap ourselves back into our reality – which, in most cases, is never as good as what we daydream about.

So why don't we just pursue those daydreams? What's stopping us?

The answer is that simple, but powerful, four-letter word:

FEAR

We are scared to death. We are afraid of change, of risks, of all the "what ifs." For whatever reason, we approach our future with a "glass half-empty" attitude, typically ingrained in us since childhood. Admonitions like "Don't run with scissors, you'll poke your eye out" still echo in our ears as adults. So we play it safe. And safe means sticking with the status quo.

Many people hand out advice on getting past fear, suggesting that once you break free from its shackles, you will be unstoppable. That sounds good on the surface, but it's a little more complex than that.

Yes, it's important to master fear to feel free and move on, but fear can also be our friend. Fear provides an excellent entrée to opportunity. Think about it:

- Do you get flustered and tongue-tied when you meet that special someone?

- Do you get nervous making a presentation to the CEO of your company or your peers?

- What's worse – the thought of failing at your daydream job, or of failing at some temp job?

What's the common theme in these questions? Fear guides you and shows you what is really important; what matters to you. That's why you get nervous – you don't want to blow it. If you didn't have fear to help identify the things you want, you might not know how to make that distinction.

Furthermore, fear motivates us to take action. Thousands of years ago, cave dwellers ran away from wild animals, driven by their strong instinct for self-preservation. In today's world, our fears are not caused by threats from menacing beasts, but rather by thoughts of losing our jobs, homelessness, hunger, being separated from our loved ones, *etc.*

In these cases, our fear motivates us to get out of bed every day to make a living, which enhances our odds of being able to afford food and housing, and have a reasonable quality of life. In other words, fear provides us with the energy and motivation to do what needs to be done to ensure our (metaphorical) survival.

Fear is also a powerful motivator insomuch as it relates to our loved ones. We would do anything to guarantee the health, safety, and welfare of our family. We prove that every day by doing tasks that are a direct reflection of how we are strongly motivated by love.

For example, even though parents of a newborn might be exhausted and don't feel like getting up in the middle of the night to feed their baby (again!), they do it anyway, of course. Their love for their child is stronger than the desire to stay in their warm comfy bed and go back to sleep.

The sacrifices and commitment we make for our loved ones continue throughout our lives as we raise children, extend our love and assistance to friends and family members in need, and care for our aging parents.

When fear rears its ugly head consistently over time, however, we are unable to achieve goals because fear fuels repeated bouts of disappointment or failure. And failure creates more fear and paralyzes our actions.

Here are but a few of the reasons why we fail:

We fail when we are not true to ourselves.

That is, we do not value our uniqueness and all that we have to offer. We may not realize the tremendous potential inside of us until we accept that we are uniquely special, have distinct skill sets and talents that no one else has, and are loved by people who will support us along the way.

We fail when we feel sorry for ourselves.

Self-pity keeps us from trying, or from believing we deserve better. When we feel bad for ourselves, it suppresses our self-esteem, shatters our confidence, and leads us to believe we are being punished when we fail. As a result, we give up, lose faith, retreat into a "safe place" and resist anything that will expose us to risk.

THE FEAR FACTOR

We fail because of a lack of effort.

Many times, a simple lack of effort causes us to lose momentum and drive, bringing the mission to a grinding halt. All things in life worth having require work – they don't usually just fall into our laps haphazardly. We have to go after them. Applying effort and hard work requires us to learn something new and do things outside of our comfort zones.

We fail because we complain.

If things seem too difficult or unfair, we complain instead of accepting the challenge and forging ahead. We crawl into a negative zone, get angry, pout like a child, and then stop trying. We blame others instead of owning up to our shortcomings or lack of resolve, and taking responsibility for our actions.

We fail because we do not believe.

As strange as it sounds, sometimes we sabotage our efforts due to a lack of confidence or belief in ourselves. That forces us to come up with excuses so that the blame is directed elsewhere. Because we don't firmly believe that we are capable of succeeding at something, it's easier to stay focused on the negative circumstances hindering progress, which blinds us to the possibilities for success.

SET YOURSELF FREE

We fail because we quit.

Failing because we quit, of course, is the greatest failure of all – and such an unnecessary shame. We have been taught since childhood never to quit or give up; and yet, as problems and challenges build in our complex lives, the convenient escape is just to throw up our hands and say "I'm not playing anymore." When we lose hope, we want to quit, and this defeatist attitude keeps us from picking ourselves back up and persisting until things turn around.

I am sure some of these sound familiar. Has fear kept you from living a successful and fulfilling life? Only you can make the decision to attack fear and become the successful person you were born to be. Only you can decide to change bad habits of defeat into good habits of success. No one can do it for you. It's up to you to take command of your life and begin believing the truth about who you are and your unlimited potential to succeed!

If you want to have any chance at all of reaching your potential and achieving true happiness, you must erase fear and failure from your vocabulary.

Over the years as I have traveled the world as a professional speaker, I have addressed audiences from all walks of life. Many people who have approached me after my talks have said: "I enjoyed your presentation, but in my unique and specific situation I can't pursue my daydreams because…"

THE FEAR FACTOR

When I press for more details, their replies always start with "I'm too…" They continue with words like "old," "poor," "inexperienced," "young," "uneducated," *etc.* – take your pick. But all of those reasons are usually rooted in fear.

Typically I respond with an expression that popped into my head a few years ago: "Believe in yourself and the rest will follow." That response may come across as a simplistic, unrealistic and unsatisfying comeback delivered by an optimistic person who feeds off of positive adages, but it's one I truly trust.

Now, I am not naïve enough to suggest that life is simple and people don't have real burdens and obstacles to overcome. But I do know there are many inspiring stories of people who have faced incredible odds and achieved success due to their resolve and steadfast beliefs that they could climb out of their hole.

For many of us, fear keeps us from achieving the goals, the success, the professional position, and the life we want. Sometimes it's difficult to pinpoint or name the fear. We just know it exists and aren't sure how to get past it to break through and move forward. Fear can stop us in our tracks and keep us from accepting what should be ours. And because fear is the great unknown, we can't predict the outcome, and instinctively we allow negative thoughts to enter our brains.

For example, when someone says, "I am fearful of public speaking," they do not mean they are afraid that someone in the audience will attack them physically. Rather, they are afraid of failure. If they spoke more accurately, they would say, "I am afraid of how I will feel emotionally and whether I will live up to the expectations of the audience. I am afraid of how I will look, and I am afraid that I will not do well." In other words, the fear of not being respected.

Struggling through my fears over the years, I have found that the solution is not to let the fear itself hold you back. When you put a plan together and take it one step at a time, you begin to build confidence in yourself and the plan. The more structure you have and the more positive habits you build, the less fear you will have. For me, that means rehearsing my talks over and over when I am preparing to give a speech (using a mirror) until I feel totally comfortable with what I will be saying and how I look.

In the battle against fear, it's also important to remember that you are not alone. Everyone has fears. The antidote is to face fear head-on and attack it methodically: Define whatever your fear is, reset your focus to the result, and take action toward that result. Over time you will move past what is obstructing your progress.

Here are some of the things I have learned in my battle to overcome the fears that have held me back in my life:

THE FEAR FACTOR

Assess the risk and break it down.

When faced with a big decision or risk that you are contemplating as you attempt to redefine your life/career direction, ask yourself these questions:

- What would you gain from taking the risk?
- What is frightening you about it?
- What's the worst thing that could happen if it turned out badly?
- If the worst thing happened, what would you do?
- What could you do to minimize it?
- What information would make it less risky?
- If you broke the risk down into small steps, what would be the first step?
- When could you take that step?
- What exactly are you afraid of in the process?

Digest these questions and decide whether your fear is realistic or irrational. Remember that most of the things you fear won't happen.

Taking small steps is a sensible approach for fear that seems overwhelming. Your initial reaction to fear might be to avoid what it is you are afraid of. I have found that if you can break down what you are afraid of into small steps, it bypasses the paralysis and allows you to get moving in the right direction.

When you identify your fear(s) and think about the steps you need to take to build your confidence and get motivated, you begin to make a transition into a comfort zone that allows you to build confidence.

Another approach is to think of failure simply as feedback on what you need to improve. If you listen carefully to the advice failure gives you, you will inevitably overcome those barriers and plow ahead, and success will come. I speak from personal experience. I have started four businesses, and three of them failed – but the one that succeeded has made me forget the others, and I would have never been able to find the success I am currently enjoying without the experiences gained through those failures.

In one of those risky examples, I quit my lucrative and secure job in 1999 and "dropped out" for 18 months to write and attempt to sell a TV sitcom called "Bon Voyage" to TV producers in Hollywood. I moved ahead with this project in spite of the fact that I read beforehand that the chances of selling a TV show were akin to hitting the lottery.

THE FEAR FACTOR

Undeterred, I forged ahead with the full support of my amazing wife, who became the family breadwinner while I embarked on this improbable journey. After countless setbacks and disappointments, I continued to be hopeful and confident that I was onto something big, and that it was just a matter of time until I hit pay dirt.

Alas, that never happened. Though I never lost faith in the concept, I eventually came to the conclusion that I was not going to be able to sell the show. So I accepted my fate and redirected my efforts into starting a new business, which ultimately became very prosperous.

The lessons learned along the way from my "Bon Voyage" experience continue to guide my thinking today. Bottom line: I tried and failed, but then moved on to the next thing. I'm still here; I'm still alive, and I overcame all the fears I had at the time and gave it my best shot.

The main reason I moved forward in that example was that I had read stories of people who succeeded in spite of the odds – and I chose to think positively rather than listen to the doomsday predictions of the naysayers who pointed out all the reasons why I would fail. If you let those negative influencers control your destiny, you will never get out of the gate.

Another good piece of advice I received many years ago in this context was to "live in the present." Don't let your thoughts and emotions run away to the future or the past. Being in the present means not dwelling and obsessing on what *has* gone wrong and what *could* go wrong. This runaway thinking will only heighten your fear to the point that you might feel unable to do anything. Instead, make your plans, and move forward – one step at a time.

Chapter 4

EXCUSES, EXCUSES

"There are a thousand excuses for failure, but never a good reason."

— *Mark Twain*

We talked about fear in the last chapter, which leads directly to the subject of excuses. Since childhood, we have learned to come up with convenient justifications for why we didn't meet a deadline ("The dog ate my homework"), perform basic tasks, or achieve our potential. Essentially, it boils down to the fact that most of the time we're just lazy and undisciplined.

As an example, it's always interesting to observe the annual phenomenon of New Year resolutions. Studies reveal that more than 50% of people make a list of things they will do or change in the New Year, but what's telling is how quickly they abandon their plans.

Most New Year resolutions are repeats from years past: lose weight, exercise more, eat better, change jobs, spend more time with family, *etc*. But survey results show that most of us fall away from our stated goals by the end of January, which helps explain why health clubs are so crowded during the first month of each year, then settle back to their average numbers by mid-February.

There are several reasons why we fail to stick to our resolutions and make them last throughout the year. We usually tend to start off strong with pumped-up expectations, but quickly slide back into our old ways.

After we fall off the wagon once or twice (overeating or skipping the new gym workout regimen) we toss the whole plan out the window and accept too soon that we just can't do it. We come up with handy, familiar excuses to justify our failure – too busy, too tired, too hungry, too this, too that. But, if you think about it, there is no reason to abandon our good intentions just because of a slip-up or two.

After all, it takes about 30 days to develop new habits.

If we eat a slice of pizza and break the streak of five days on a diet, that's not a reason to throw in the towel. And just because that business trip interrupted our momentum and we didn't work out for a week, we shouldn't give up and quit. We needn't be deterred if we stumble a few times along the way, as long as we are committed to the long-term goals, stay the course and get back on track.

EXCUSES, EXCUSES

We can learn a great deal about how to do this by looking at famous examples of people who did not let excuses get in their way.

In my research for this book, I came across the story of George Washington Carver, an African-American scientist, and inventor. He was born into slavery in 1861 and experienced many hardships that could have easily kept him from fulfilling his potential. A childhood disease left him frail and unable to work in the fields. Instead, his interest in plants drove him to learn as much as he could about them. He was denied admission to a university because of his race, but that didn't stop him. He kept trying and believing. He didn't allow rejection, bitterness, or injustice to thwart his drive to be his best. Excuses were not an option for him.

Five years later, he got accepted into another college. He kept pushing himself to succeed, as the burning potential inside of him would not lie dormant. Rather, he exploited his potential and, in the process, revolutionized agricultural science. Today he is well known for his many contributions, including discoveries of hundreds of uses for the peanut and other crops.

Here are a few more examples of people who did not let excuses deter them:

SET YOURSELF FREE

"It can't be done."

All the way until the middle of the twentieth century, running a four-minute mile was thought to be physically impossible, and scientists and medical experts came up with a list of reasons why it couldn't be done.

That didn't stop British runner Roger Bannister, who tossed all excuses to the side of the track on May 6, 1954 at the Iffley Road track in Oxford, England where he ran the mile in 3 minutes, 59.4 seconds. Twenty-six days later the record was broken again and has continued to fall in the decades since until reaching its current record of 3:43:13. The power of the human spirit overcame all the excuses for why it could not be done.

The story of Sir Edmund Hillary's momentous achievement a year earlier – climbing Mt. Everest – could also be included in this "Can't be done" category.

"You're never too old."

On September 2, 2013, at the age of 64, American swimmer Diana Nyad emerged onto the shore of Key West, Florida after swimming 111 miles from Havana, Cuba in an epic feat of endurance and human will. It took her an incredible 53 hours to complete her amazing accomplishment.

EXCUSES, EXCUSES

Diana carried three poignant messages on her journey across this dangerous stretch of shark-infested waters and strong currents, and spoke about them to the crowd as she made her way onto the beach, barely able to stand or talk through her exhaustion and swollen, sun-parched lips:

- Never, ever give up.

- You're never too old to chase your dreams.

- Though swimming looks like a solitary sport, it took the efforts of an entire team for her to be successful.

Millions of people around the world cheered Diana on, moved by her unstoppable tenacity to be the first to make the historic crossing without the aid of a shark cage. At the end of her glorious journey, and after 35 years and four crushing failures, the public found hope in Diana's perseverance – and her "no excuse" attitude. They were inspired by her mantra "Find a way," which led her to realize a daydream in her sixties that had eluded her as a young champion in peak form.

Another example that resonates with me in the "You're never too old" group is Ray Kroc. In 1961, when Kroc was 59 years old, he purchased a small hamburger chain in California from the McDonald brothers. As the new owner and CEO of the company, he guided the growth of

McDonald's to 7,500 outlets at the time of his death in 1984, and is credited with creating the most successful franchise system in the world. Six years before he bought the company he was a milkshake machine salesman who saw the tremendous potential to expand McDonald's nationwide. That vision and drive catapulted him to success and wealth in the twilight of his career – age was not an issue.

"You're never too down and out."

In 2007, Anne Mahlum was 26 years old and living in Philadelphia. She was at a crossroads in her life. For the past several months, she had been consumed with thoughts of what her purpose was, and was willing to do anything to find it. She just didn't know where to look. Soon she realized it was right beneath her feet.

Running was Anne's staple. She became a runner when she was 16 to get her through a turbulent family time caused by her father's gambling addiction. She found clarity and strength in the movement of running. It helped her to understand that you must take things one step at a time. It also helped her to realize that some roads lead to difficult choices – you either persevere or turn around and make excuses. Running helped Anne discover who she was and what she loved about herself.

Ten years later, in May of 2007 at 5:30 a.m. one morning on the streets of Philadelphia, Anne interrupted her morning run to talk to several homeless men outside a rescue mission. During her conversations with them, she realized that she could help these people if she stopped running *by* them and started running *with* them.

With some determination, purpose and persistence, she began an official running club with nine of the men who frequented the shelter. She got some of her friends to donate new running shoes and outfitted them with running clothes and socks. On July 3, 2007, their first one-mile run took place. Within a week, the group grew, and ten more people stepped forward as volunteers.

The morning runs created a community that respected equality and promoted and rewarded positive behavior. Friendships were formed, and smiles were constant. During this time, Anne made two powerful observations that helped her realize that her growing community could be so much more than just a running club – it could be the foundation to change people's lives.

The club members were coming out every day of their volition, and Anne believed that voluntary behavior was the only way the change was possible. No one was forcing or threatening them to be on that corner at 6:00 a.m. They were there because they wanted to be. No excuses.

While the members' times were being recorded after each morning's run, each runner waited anxiously to get the results and receive credit for their hard work. It became clear to Anne and the volunteers that no matter how many differences there are between us, the similarities are what connect us and make us human. We all want to be noticed, appreciated, recognized, valued, cared for and loved. It is these emotions that drive each of us every day.

The question that Anne asked herself was, "If we can change the way people see themselves, can we change the direction of their lives?" She felt very strongly that if she and her volunteer team could help these homeless people see themselves as deserving, capable, hardworking, responsible, disciplined, focused and reliable, it would be possible for them to move toward independence.

Realizing that she had an incredible opportunity to change their lives, she made a life/career-altering decision to quit her job and formed a non-profit she named Back on My Feet. (www.backonmyfeet.org)

Since its launch in 2007, Back on My Feet has served more than 5,500 individuals experiencing (or at risk of) homelessness, and has engaged more than 100,000 volunteers and supporters. At any given time, 80% of BOMF members are participating in the organization's Next Steps program, which works to secure employment and housing. More than 1,500 members have completed their GED, taken up further education or completed certified vocational training.

Through it all, Anne and the members of the running community she formed in the shadow of her insecurities have learned the valuable lesson that excuses can be overcome with hope, tenacity and hard work.

Chapter 5

CHOICES

"We all make choices,
but in the end our choices make us."

—*Andrew Ryan*

Ryan's quote is simple but quite profound. It is a fact that we all have our free will – the ability to voluntarily decide to perform one or more of several possible acts or to avoid action entirely. Rooted in these choices are the future consequences of our selections, good or bad.

Many times we choose to think first before we act, and end up pleased with the outcome. But there are other times when we make the wrong choice because we act without thinking, or because our life circumstances at that moment distract us from the right course.

Choices vary from situation to situation – and there is always the choice to do nothing – but the decision still lies with us. So, in making those decisions, we have to be very careful because where we are and who we are is directly related to the choices we make.

It is safe to say that we usually want the best for our lives and are inclined to do all the things we need to do to succeed. We can never possess something we desire unless we plan and work hard for it. We own the key to our goals and daydreams. For example, we can get good grades in school only if we choose to prioritize, study hard and stay focused.

When we choose to take shortcuts, or not put in the work, or simply goof off – then the consequences are predictable. I learned this the hard way in high school. Though I was smart enough and had the capacity to excel, I chose to have fun instead of studying – and my grades suffered. Ultimately I failed a physics class in my senior year and was not allowed to walk with my fellow students at the graduation ceremony. To get my diploma, I had to go to summer school to complete the course.

I hated my teacher at the time for failing me, and blamed the pain I felt on the night of my graduation on him. I vividly recall sitting in my bedroom at home in tears because I wasn't with my friends, but the experience forced me to take a close look at my behavior, actions, and bad choices. Today I look back and thank that teacher for the bitter medicine he prescribed, which helped steer me back on the right course.

Interestingly and ironically enough, one of the things I do remember from that physics class was Isaac Newton's *Third Law of Motion*. You may be familiar with it:

"For every action, there is an equal and opposite reaction."

It's a scientific law in the universe, and that law includes every part of your life: from the work you do, to your family, friends and other people, and your opinion of yourself.

You are responsible for your life. *You* create and sustain your life. Every thought, word, action, and *choice* that you make also has an equal *reaction*. For example, if you are a kind person – interested in giving to and helping others – then your actions will have a good effect, or good "re-action" on others (and also on you). If your actions are corrupt and disrespectful to others, then you will hurt people and hurt yourself as well. Simply put – like attracts like.

If your life is not going the way you wanted or expected it to go, you can look at the choices you have made along the way as the biggest contributor to your current state. Conversely, if things are going (for the most part) as you planned, the good choices you made positioned you for the life you are leading.

The good news is that it's never too late to start making changes and good choices in your life. Regardless of the situation you are in, you can change your life and perspective of the world at any moment. You *can* make new choices, *different* choices, and *better* choices at any time to improve your life in a myriad of positive ways.

So if misery, pain, and loneliness are working well for you, keep going. *Or*, make new choices and proceed in a new direction. You have the power. You're in control of your life.

In Ernest Henley's famous poem "Invictus" he says:

"I am the master of my fate; I am the captain of my soul."

You are in charge of your future journey. Your destiny is in your hands. It's not haphazard – not hit or miss. It's *your* choice. So choose wisely.

Chapter 6

THE PROCRASTINATION TRAP

> "Never put off until tomorrow,
> what you can do today."
>
> — *Thomas Jefferson*

Ah, procrastination! That evil and nagging devil that whispers in our ear that putting something off until later is perfectly acceptable. We all fall prey to classic avoidance instincts and then feel guilty day after day when we can't complete the task at hand.

According to Wikipedia, the definition of procrastination is:

"The avoidance of doing a task which needs to be accomplished. It is the practice of doing more pleasurable things in place of less pleasurable ones or carrying out less urgent tasks instead of more urgent ones, thus putting off impending tasks to a later time. Sometimes, procrastination takes place until the 'last minute' before a deadline.

Procrastination can take hold of any aspect of life – putting off cleaning the stove, repairing a leaky roof, seeing a doctor or dentist, submitting a job report or academic assignment, or broaching a stressful issue with a partner. It can lead to feelings of guilt, inadequacy, depression and self-doubt."

Procrastination is a universal bane of life. We all procrastinate at one time or another. Some folks are chronic procrastinators, while others put things off intermittently because they have taken on too many tasks, forcing the completion of some of them to take a back seat.

People put things off until tomorrow, and when tomorrow comes they put them off until the next day. Writing this book is a prime example of this. It has taken me more than a year to complete it. Because I did not stay true to my self-imposed deadlines, I allowed myself to drift further and further away from my completion target date. Granted, there were legitimate reasons why I was interrupted, but when those other commitments had been fulfilled, procrastination reared its ugly head again.

When I could have and should have been writing the book, I found myself latching on to flimsy excuses such as "writer's block" to put it off even further. To be frank, many times it was simply the excuse mentioned previously – lack of focus and discipline.

SET YOURSELF FREE

We sometimes forget that by procrastinating, we're only hurting ourselves. With procrastination comes a delay in receiving the rewards of reaching the end goal.

In my case, I delayed the opportunity to get this book into the marketplace earlier, and to derive income from my work. That impacted my ability to book more speaking jobs as a published author, which directly impacted my pocketbook. And I consider myself a motivated person! It just goes to prove that consistent hard work, focus and discipline are all required to get you to your final destination, and you can't let procrastination be a deterrent.

When we loop this conversation back to "Daydream it… Believe it… Achieve it," we have to be realistic and recognize that you may have to deal with your procrastination as you set your goals to make the desired changes in your life.

One of the things that allowed me to get back on track and finish this book was recalibrating the process. By that I mean I simply started from scratch and put a new timeline in place, while making a commitment to myself to follow it *via* a detailed plan with milestone timelines established.

The good news in my situation was the fact that I wasn't starting from the beginning – the book was already half written. And because I had a tangible document in my hands, it was easier for me to visualize what the finished book would look like this time around than it was when I first sat down to write it a year ago (in front of a blank computer screen.)

By putting a new plan together with realistic dates and times blocked off on my calendar, I was ready to tackle the project in earnest with a renewed enthusiasm and drive. And it worked. You are reading the book, right?

Here are some of the things that I incorporated into my plan that helped me, which I suggest you consider in your planning process:

Commit to doing at least ONE thing a day towards completing your goal.

Regardless of how busy you are, set aside 15–30 minutes a day (minimum) to concentrate on finishing at least one task that will allow you to keep the process moving.

Avoid distractions and diversions.

For me, I have numerous hobbies and spend a lot of time watching TV and movies – which cut into my writing time. By eliminating some of the time spent on those diversions, and redirecting them towards the book, I was able to get more done.

Focus on the prize!

Think back to how your daydream initially got you pumped up and excited about reaching that goal. Not unlike Olympic athletes, it's important to maintain that vision to stay on track. Keep your eye on the pay-off and visualize how happy you will be when you finally reach your target.

Stop waiting for tomorrow.

Sometimes we allow ourselves to push the task back "just a day," perhaps convinced that tomorrow would be better because "I'll be well rested," or "I won't be as busy," or some other false excuse. And then when tomorrow comes, the same thing happens – we push it back again to the following day. Do not fall for that mental scam your brain plays on you.

Don't rationalize the delay.

Our reasons for procrastinating take many forms, and we try to justify the holdup by weighing the consequences of the delay versus the benefits of achieving the desired result.

For example, when we are trying to get back into shape, we might quit our workout routine in the fall using the rationale that we'll have plenty of time to get in shape in the spring when swimsuit season is approaching. That's just another mind trick.

To summarize: Beware the Procrastination Trap. There are many roadblocks to achieving our daydreams, but one of the most sure-fire ways to derail our efforts is to succumb to procrastination. It's a form of self-sabotage that puts unnecessary obstacles in our path. Don't let procrastination hold you back!

Chapter 7

WORK-LIFE BALANCE

"We work to live, not live to work."
— *Michael Lyons*

When I was a small child (before I began school), I asked my Dad why he had to go to work each day. He told me that he had to work so we could have money to buy all the things we needed to live. His response seemed reasonable, but all I knew is that I wanted him to stay home all day and play with my little sister and me. I truly treasured – even at that young age – the precious time I spent with him and my Mom.

When they weren't working (my Mom was a busy housewife), they were taking care of all the other things they were responsible for in a family that eventually grew to six kids. Early on, I realized that there was a lot of "stuff" that had to be crammed into a day, and yet all I selfishly wanted was for them to spend time with me.

WORK-LIFE BALANCE

Back then, the world seemed a simpler place, and in spite of the daily duties that confronted them, we never lacked in love nor care from our parents. They always found time to help us with our school lessons, throw a ball around in the backyard, or play games like chess or Monopoly. We spent many evenings reading to each other and enjoying just being together as a family. Education and learning were a priority in our family, and my Dad, in particular, was always exposing us to a wide variety of experiences from poetry, to fencing, to museum outings.

Looking back, I realize now that they, like us, had to figure out a way to balance the demands of their responsibilities with the joy of raising their children in an environment that nurtured a sense of well-being and happiness. I also recognize how blessed we were to have two loving parents and admire all the sacrifices they made for us. Admittedly there weren't as many distractions for them as there are now, but they did an outstanding job of balancing their work and personal lives.

Today, this whole concept of work–life balance which I positively experienced as a child, appears to be threatened in our complex, fast-moving world. It seems we live to work instead of the other way around – and in the end, our personal development and relationships suffer. In my opinion, this may be why we see so many dysfunctional people in the world today with serious issues that don't allow them to lead "normal" lives.

Somewhere along the way they did not receive what my siblings and I got from our parents: good guidance, firm discipline, and plenty of attention and love. Perhaps they have been victims of many complicated events that occurred in their lives. The daily struggles of many parents, for example, may not allow them the freedom or as much time to devote to their children as they would like, leaving a void that manifests itself in problematic childhood behaviors that exacerbate as they get older.

The term "work–life balance" has become a 21st-century buzz phrase and preoccupation. We think about it, know it's a challenge, but aren't exactly sure how to tackle it. Our lives are so complex, and we are running so fast, that we struggle to maintain a healthy balance in our lives. We beat ourselves up constantly wondering whether we are devoting enough time to what I call all the "als" in our life – mental, physical, social, spiritual, financial, emotional, medical, *etc.* – that make us who we are.

And the main culprit that jumps out at me that has disrupted our ability to balance those "als" like our parents did in "the good old days," is the advent of electronic distractions.

It started way back when with radio, then TV, and then as time went on, video games and other diversionary toys were added to the list. Little by little, they all conspired to take big chunks out of our precious family time, and now it has gotten completely out of hand. Computers, tablets, smartphones and other gadgets gobble up our waking moments, endorsed by a new culture that not only accepts this new behavior but embraces it.

Call me old-fashioned, but I see this disturbing trend, which has been brewing in our society over the past few years, to be destructive and dangerous. As we have become more and more reliant on technology, our personal relationships with family and friends have suffered because we are all walking around with our heads down looking at our devices, lessening our face-to-face contact.

I am sure that like me when you are out in public you have seen the following scenarios:

- Young couples and families in a restaurant who take out their smartphones to check messages, emails, and social networks even before looking at the menu, and then constantly check their phones during the meal, barely paying attention to each other.

- People crossing the street, or worse - driving their cars - while their eyes are on their phones instead of on the road, which has become a dangerous common occurrence.

- Toddlers in strollers playing with a digital device — a parent's or perhaps even their own — instead of observing and learning from the world around them. These gadgets have become convenient electronic baby-sitters as parents use them as a way to calm disruptive children and keep them from interrupting their own screen activities!

As with anything else in life, moderation regarding our use of technology devices should be the standard of a healthy relationship with these tools. Too many of us have become slaves to the devices that were supposed to free us, giving us more time to experience life and the people we love. Instead, we're constantly bombarded by bells, buzzes and chimes that alert us to messages we feel compelled to view and respond to immediately.

Not too long ago I read an article that stated most people check their smartphones roughly 150 times per day (about every six minutes.) And young adults are averaging 110 texts per day. These stats should make us stop and think. Are we turning into digital robots? What kind of impact will this behavior have on future generations? Will they know how to converse with one another face to face? Will they notice what is going on around them? Will they appreciate a beautiful sunrise, the chirping of birds, and the people with whom they share the planet?

I do not dispute that the advances in technology have created efficient and useful information and communication instruments – but they are competing head-on with face-to-face interaction at a rapid pace, whether we like it or not.

The horse is already out of the barn, so it's not logical to think we are going to put down our devices and swear off technology altogether. But the fact remains that there is no substitute for human face-to-face communication, and we should not gloss over that reality. What is often missed when discussing this subject is the importance of body language when people are together in person.

Studies show that only 7% of communication is transmitted *via* the written or verbal word, meaning that an astounding 93% is attributed to non-verbal body language. It is only when we are face-to-face that we can interpret the tone of a voice instantly or look into someone's eyes to deduce whether "It's all good" really means all *is* actually good, or whether it's a dubious statement. In person, we have a number of cues available in addition to the words themselves – facial expressions, gestures, body language, and voice tone – which complement the words and the message.

But when communicating online, we lose that ability to accurately assess the other person's receptiveness and emotional response to the dialogue. And this presents an unprecedented paradox: With all the powerful social technologies at our fingertips, we are more connected – and yet potentially more disconnected – than ever before.

Every relevant metric I have seen indicates that we are interacting at breakneck speed and frequency through social media. But at what cost? Is communication now about rapid responses instead of thoughtful, measured exchanges? Are we really *communicating*? With 93% of the communication context removed, we are attempting to build relationships and draw conclusions based on short phrases, abbreviations, and emojis – which may or may not accurately represent the sender's message.

To make it worse, social media and technology have blurred the traditional barriers of space and time, creating a 24/7 world that poses a threat to the time-honored boundaries between our work life and personal life.

Ironically, social media is making us less social – and has become a substitute for the real thing.

The other issue is that because most communication is now done *via* emails, texts, instant messaging, and other technology-enabled media (without the benefit of body language), the potential for misunderstanding increases. In our high-stress, constantly rushed state of mind, we don't always take the time to read and re-read each communication before hitting "Send," and the subtle nuances of the message may be misinterpreted.

Not only has this created a serious dilemma in the workplace, but more importantly, it has also seeped into our personal lives with alarming impact. We have all probably sent an email or text on our smartphone, checked Facebook, or talked on the phone while in the presence of family members. Sometimes it seems impossible to avoid the constant connectivity that life in this century demands. But is this need to connect affecting our connection to the very people we love the most?

Studies have shown that children, in particular, feel that parents pay less attention to them than to their smartphones (and, admittedly, *vice versa*) – especially at mealtimes, in the car, or while attending events.

I contend that none of us want to create a chasm in our family relationships, so we must make a conscious effort to modify our behavior. It may be hard to break the habit, but resisting the temptation to grab that device every five minutes while in the presence of loved ones, and spend more genuine face-to-face time with them without distraction or interruptions, is not a bad idea.

SET YOURSELF FREE

Simply stated, if we care about and value our relationships – as we all should – each one of us has to do our part by making adjustments in our daily online conduct, and by encouraging as much face-to-face interaction as possible with all the people in our lives – both on a personal and professional level.

Be in the moment. Be present. And feed all the "als" in your life to create a strong work–life balance that will contribute to your overall happiness and state of mind.

Chapter 8

THE BRAND OF YOU

"You are the CEO of Me, Inc."

— *Tom Peters*

Personal happiness and success in your chosen field of work go hand in hand, and how you manage your personal brand - or what I like to call the "Brand of You" - directly influences both. As a speaker, this is the talk I deliver the most. The subject matter resonates with audiences of all ages, experience levels, and demographics because we all have a personal brand, and how you project and polish that brand every day goes a long way in determining the degree of your success.

Enhancing your personal brand is not optional – rather, it is essential for the advancement of your career, improvement as a leader, and becoming a better person.

Developing the "Brand of You" is an ongoing responsibility - a never-ending journey that requires a full-time commitment to how you define yourself, make good decisions, and serve as an exemplary role model to the people around you.

Your personal brand should represent the value you are consistently able to deliver to those whom you are serving. This doesn't mean self-promotion. Rather, you should view your personal brand as a trademark - similar to iconic brands like Apple or Disney – and treat it as an asset that must be protected while continuously shaping it. And it must be managed with the intention of helping others benefit from having a relationship with you, and by being associated with you and your work.

Successful companies are masters at branding. Their brands imply value, quality, consistency and a positive image - with results to match. When talking about the "Brand of You," the same characteristics apply.

So the first question is: Have you defined your personal brand? And if so, are you consistently living your brand every day?

If you're like most people, your answer to both questions is no. It is estimated that less than 15% of people have truly defined their personal brand and less than 5% are living it consistently – each and every day. Why? Probably because it requires conscious thought, self-awareness, action, and accountability.

So exactly *what is* a personal brand? One way to describe it is this: it is the total experience of someone having a relationship with who you are, and what you represent as an individual. Think about what that means. Ask yourself, and then ask a close friend, what is the total experience of having a relationship with you like?

An exercise I conduct in the seminars I deliver is to pair people up who know each other. I then ask one person to write down five words to describe the other person, and *vice versa,* while also writing five words to describe themselves. When they are finished, I ask them to compare notes. In all the times I have done this, I have never once seen all five words match up. That is because we perceive ourselves differently than how others perceive us.

Through my research, I have come across dozens of definitions of what a personal brand is. The one that captures it best for me is this one from Intrinsic Genius:

"The unfair advantage every individual has by capturing the Value of our Personal Characteristics, Attributes and Life Experiences in a package that we effectively communicate to our audience, leveraging the specific 'use value' that comes from our Unique Talent." ~ Intrinsic Genius

What I like most about this particular description is the "unfair advantage" part. Essentially it says that because each of us possesses a unique package of traits and skills, when we leverage that advantage by harnessing our special talents, it gives us an exclusive opportunity to distinguish ourselves from others who may appear, on the surface, to be similar.

But you have to work it! Think about this: Every time you are out in public, or in a meeting, or at an event; your brand is on display. Like it or not, every person you come into contact with is judging you – either positively or negatively – based on how you behave, communicate, respond, look, and most importantly whether you are "likable."

When I say "likable," I mean do you come across as approachable, pleasant and friendly? Do people, upon meeting you, get the feeling they can trust you? Do you project an image of confidence and competence?

In every interaction, you should be mindful of what others are experiencing about you and what *you* want others to experience about you. Each of these engagements is similar to a job interview – except in these cases, you are being evaluated by your peers. Those who know how to live and manage their personal brand will earn their respect in any situation.

At first, this may seem like a bit of a challenge. However, when you start to see yourself through the lens of a brand, your perspective will change, and you will become more mindful about how you approach the personal brand you are trying to project and live.

You should not confuse your brand with "acting a part," or faking what your true brand is. To the contrary, you should focus on being your authentic *real* self while constantly striving to improve your persona. As discussed in the first chapter of this book, keep in mind that we have been conditioned to want to be more like others. Therefore, we are more likely to feel accountable to others and what *they* want us to be, rather than being true to ourselves.

If people you come into contact with don't know what your personal brand is, the fault is yours - not theirs.

Here are some methods to build an awesome personal brand:

Start thinking of yourself as a brand

What do you wish people to associate with you when they think of your name? If you could make a list of the attributes you'd like to have to represent your personal brand – what would they be? In your line of work is there a certain subject matter in which you want to be perceived as an expert, or are there general qualities you want to be linked to your brand? Once you understand how you wish your brand to be perceived, you can start to be much more strategic about building it.

SET YOURSELF FREE

Audit your online presence

You can't mold perception without first understanding your current status. What comes up when you Google yourself? Have you posted anything on social media that is inappropriate or embarrassing? Your digital footprint in this day and age is out there and, in many cases, cannot be retrieved if you want to erase it.

Cultivating a strong personal brand is just as much about being responsive to what is being said as it is about creating intellectual property.

Create a personal website and use LinkedIn

In this digital age, it is important to take advantage of the tools available to build your brand.

Depending on what you do for a living, creating and maintaining a website might be a valuable and necessary part of your promotional efforts. In my case, a website is an essential part of my marketing toolkit as an actor and speaker.

I bought the URL www.michaeljlyons.com about 16 years ago and just sat on it, knowing in my gut that someday I would finally be out on my own and would need to market myself. When the time came, I populated it with content designed to familiarize the reader with my brand and offerings.

Having a personal website is also one of the best ways to get a good rank for your name on search engines. And it doesn't need to be robust. It can be a simple two or three page site with your resume, link to your social platforms, and a brief bio. You can always expand the website with additional subject matter and continue to update it regularly as you add new and relevant information.

LinkedIn has become a "must-have" for all professionals. Chances are you already have a LinkedIn page and if you don't, stop reading this book and go set one up immediately.

When used properly and on a regular basis, LinkedIn offers features and benefits too numerous to mention. But it is very important that you do the following:

- Complete your profile with as much information as possible.

- Post a picture (smile!)

- Work your recommendations – both ways!

- Stay up-to-date on what's happening in your connections' worlds.

- Start a conversation.

- Share posts at least every two months.

Find ways to create value

We've all been there. Someone in your network posts something utterly mundane or ridiculous, and you wonder what compelled them to do so? A medium is not a substitute for a message. Find ways to add value to your audience by creating or curating content that's in line with your brand. Whether it be on Facebook, Twitter or other social media, make sure the information you put out there is relevant and useful. That goes a long way in helping to establish you as a thought leader and enhances your credibility.

Be purposeful in what you share

Every tweet you send, every status update you make, every picture you share, contributes to your personal brand. It is an amalgamation of multiple daily actions. And every single one of those communications will cause a reaction on the part of the reader: either they will find the information interesting, compelling and valuable, or they will question your motives, logic, intentions or rationale for passing it on. Either way, they will contribute to the perception of your brand.

Associate with other strong brands

This is especially true in your professional life but applies equally to your personal life as well. Your personal brand is strengthened or weakened by your connection to other personal brands. Seek out and leverage your relationship with other solid brands which can help to elevate your brand.

You may have heard the saying "he was hanging out with the wrong crowd." Being associated with the wrong crowd automatically colors the perception of your brand (in a bad way), even if you didn't do or say anything wrong. Conversely, when you are associated with individuals who are viewed in a positive light, your brand basks in the reflection of those people.

Take an active role in cultivating the opportunities to capitalize on relationships you have established in school, within your company or with colleagues you trust.

If you went to college, which school did you attend? Are there groups you can join or an alumni newsletter you can contribute to that will enhance your brand image?

What hidden opportunities are available within your company which you have yet to tap? Consider submitting a guest post to the company blog or look at other digital assets you can connect to your brand.

Who are some of your company or industry's movers and shakers that you should get to know so that you will be perceived as someone who associates with the "right people."

SET YOURSELF FREE

Reinvent Yourself

Whether you are pursuing a daydream or have suddenly found yourself out of work, you may have to chart new waters bravely – or to put it differently – reinvent yourself. This implies rethinking and repositioning your personal brand.

Over the past decade, I have known or read about several people who have taken charge of their lives and changed careers or went back to school to pursue a degree in a field unrelated to their previous work. And I applaud them all. It takes courage to change your life story in midstream.

As an example, my wife Lorie had a nursing degree and worked in that field for decades. Eventually, she yearned to do something different, and after mulling over new career options, she selected real estate. Once she made her choice, she threw herself 100% into it, studied for and received her real estate license, and had a successful run before retiring to spend more time with our grandchildren and pursue other activities.

We can draw inspiration from some exemplary celebrity brands we are all familiar with such as Oprah Winfrey, J.K. Rowling, and Sir Richard Branson. Each of them had to overcome huge obstacles before they found success, but they believed in themselves and did not allow impediments to keep them from their mission.

All of them had challenging times. Richard Branson has described his childhood this way: "I was dyslexic. I had no understanding of schoolwork whatsoever. I certainly would have failed IQ tests. It was one of the reasons I left school when I was 15 years old." But, undeterred, he founded Virgin Records at the age of 21, which eventually grew into the Virgin Group which today consists of over 400 companies. He is one of the world's most recognized and admired people - a multi-billionaire totally devoted to his family, employees, and philanthropy.

What drives him? When he formed Virgin Atlantic Airways, he was asked why he wanted to compete in the notoriously volatile aviation industry. He responded: "My interest in life comes from setting myself huge, apparently unachievable challenges and trying to rise above them. From the perspective of wanting to live life to the fullest, I felt that I had to attempt it." Today Virgin Airlines is a very successful enterprise, like most of his businesses.

J.K. Rowling was divorced, the mother of a young child, on welfare and utterly depressed when she wrote the manuscript for *"Harry Potter and the Philosopher's Stone."* She is quoted as saying "I was the worst failure I ever knew." Today, she is known the world over, has one of the most respected personal brands on the planet, and is a multi-billionaire as well.

Oprah Winfrey – who may have the strongest personal brand of them all – had to climb out of a very difficult childhood to finally become the successful entrepreneur and trendsetter that she is today.

You may not be aware of her background: She was born into poverty in rural Mississippi to a teenage single mother, and later raised in an inner-city Milwaukee neighborhood. She has stated that she was molested during her childhood and early teens and became pregnant at age 14 (her son died in infancy). Shortly after that, she was sent to Tennessee to live with the man she calls her father. While there in high school, she landed a job in radio and began co-anchoring the local evening news at the age of 19. Her emotional ad-lib delivery eventually got her transferred to the daytime-talk-show arena, and after boosting a third-rated local Chicago talk show to first place, she launched her production company and became internationally syndicated. The rest is history.

For Oprah, Branson, and Rowling – and for all of us – we are judged on our personal brand every day. If you are likable and people feel they can trust you, they will want to associate and do business with you.

Remember – It's always show time, and you are always on display: There is no such thing as a transaction that doesn't count. Your day-to-day behaviors are what shape the perception of your personal brand:

- How you deal with people

- How you make decisions

- What your work habits are

- What you seem to be good/bad at

As Tom Peters says, "You are the CEO of 'Me, Inc.'" Your career and life are in your hands. You are not defined by your title nor confined by a job description. It is your personal brand that helps to distinguish you from others. Protect it at all costs and never stop enhancing it.

Be Aware of and Polish Your Communication Skills

Over the past ten years or so, there has been a deterioration of social skills, and more and more people lack the ability to speak clearly, articulately, and intelligently - and look someone in the eye without feeling uneasy. Much of this I attribute to the rising dependence on digital devices, and an unwillingness to learn fundamental communication skills.

I have observed first-hand and on a regular basis the ill-effects of this disturbing cultural shift. In both professional and personal environments, the decline of verbal communication skills, particularly among the younger generations, has become prevalent. I cringe when I hear

"She goes" or "He's like" inserted as convenient fillers into every sentence, sprinkled with a bunch of "Uhms" and "Ahs." For some inexplicable reason, the word "like" has become an acceptable slang term, constantly overused and misused. Not only does this verbal garbage fracture the English language, but it is a direct reflection of your personal brand.

Forgive my soap box speech on this subject, but for those of you that recognize you may be a guilty party, I urge you to be cognizant of this flaw, and take action to correct it. The ability to communicate well, and properly, is a much sought-after and valued skill that employers seek in their recruitment efforts.

Chapter 9

JUST DO IT!

> "The only man who never makes mistakes
> is the man who never does anything."
> — *Theodore Roosevelt*

The three words that are now legendary in the history of global marketing – Nike's "Just do it!" – encompass a simple but powerful credo that has been the siren call to greatness for more than 25 years. Countless clothing items, shoes, print ads, billboards and TV commercials have carried that message across the planet, and it remains as potent today as it was when it was first launched as Nike's new tagline all those years ago.

One of the reasons this slogan resonates with most people is that it essentially invites us to the "Can" side of the equation, rather than the "Can't" side. It beckons us to take action. It challenges us to push ourselves. It teases us into believing that we, too, can be like Michael Jordan, or the sports superstar *du jour*.

SET YOURSELF FREE

"Can" and "Can't" are the two words that are the driving force behind either success or failure. Whereas "Can" is a word of power, "Can't" is a word of retreat. And only you have the power to decide whether you want to go for it and shoot for the stars, or slink back into your easy chair and resume playing your video game.

As we discussed earlier in the book, when you believe, and you visualize and speak positive words like "I can," you enhance your chances dramatically of attaining your goals.

If you speak with successful people, they will tell you that at the beginning of their journey, many of their acquaintances told them they would fail (just as I experienced when I started my acting career). But they (and I) ignored those negative missives and forged ahead.

The key is to realize that the most important person you need to listen to – who speaks to you every day – is *you*! If you talk to yourself in positive terms and allow that attitude to propel you, you will succeed. If you listen to negative thoughts that fill you with doubt, you will fail.

Your intuition and instincts will guide you, and your internal compass will let you know whether you are lost or on the right path. It's very easy to get detoured by negative stimuli that seep into your psyche if you are not strong enough to repel them.

JUST DO IT!

"Just do it" means getting up every morning with a positive "can do" attitude and visualizing yourself having a winning day. This in spite of the many trials and curveballs life throws our way.

You also have to be honest with yourself. Ask yourself, "Am I listening to my victory words or letting defeatist words control my outcome?" Simply said, art will not materialize, life will not get organized, and connections will not be made, if you are not taking conscious action steps, large and small, with consistency.

In this day and age, we are at a critical point where those who lack self-discipline will be eaten alive by the deluge of distractions that grow with each passing day.

When it comes to taking action over a certain period, whether that be starting a business, writing a book, or painting a canvas, we know we will not always feel motivated to do what we need to do at the moment. After all, we are human.

Here are a few things that I try to practice on a daily basis that can pay dividends on your productivity and quality of work *if* you do them regularly. You'll find that many of these actions will encourage you to push ahead with some others, as your positive "Just do it" attitude expands.

Get out of bed early.

I know. You're a night owl, and you like to work (or watch TV) deep into the night and sleep in until the last moment. But it has been scientifically proven that humans function better cognitively when it's light outside. We're strongly influenced by the cyclical nature of the Sun's interplay with the Earth. Get into the habit of getting up earlier – close to dawn, ideally. With a good previous night's sleep, you'll be more effective and more productive for a longer period.

Plan your day.

It's hard to have the clarity you need on how best to spend your time when you don't have an outline of how your day is structured.

Spending a few minutes each day writing out a plan of the actions to be taken, in their specific order, for the next day will give you this clarity. This includes recreational activities as well as chores and errands, and taking personal breaks as well (work–life balance).

If you create your "next-day plan" the night before and sleep on it, your subconscious gets a head start working on it so it's fresh on your mind when you wake up, and you're ready to attack the day with vigor.

JUST DO IT!

Set distraction-free work time zones.

This was hard for me initially, but I realized I had attention-deficit disorder, and my daily tasks were not being completed in the right order of priority. I was easily distracted by incoming emails and phone calls, which caused me to switch gears with the result that it sometimes took me hours to circle back to the tasks I started in the morning.

I now set aside specific times during the day to do emails, make phone calls, eat, work on projects, *etc*. It has made me so much more efficient and effective. I have learned that creative work and distractions do not go well together, something I believe we can all relate to. It's vital that you are disciplined about the distractions surrounding you that are harming your ability to work properly.

When you set aside distinct blocks of time, every day, in which you do nothing other than the work you need to be doing, you'll get to your end goal faster, and with less stress.

Don't worry too much about setting results targets, such as "I am going to write 1,000 words a day," because that could affect quality and process. I find that if you are truly undistracted, and totally focused on the work; you can produce what you are capable of to the best of your ability. You'll be surprised how effective you can be when you compartmentalize your work in this way.

Read over your goals.

Get into the habit of reading (and tweaking) your daydream goals and aspirations on a regular basis. By reviewing your road map and measuring and tracking your progress, you will keep yourself motivated, more centered and more driven.

Set aside time for administrative tasks.

I am a one-man band – a solo entrepreneur with no assistants or support resources. So that means I perform all the necessary functions to operate my business: pay the bills, prepare invoices, make travel arrangements, handle the marketing and sales, *etc.* It is, therefore, imperative that I organize my work to stay focused and sane.

I try to set aside a clearly defined period each week to manage administrative chores and get myself organized. When doing so, it's important to stay within the time boundaries you set for yourself, or you will end up encroaching on other work demands.

Set aside play time.

This ties into the work–life balance discussion. It is, in my opinion, important to carve out "me" time. Each day before I begin my work, my wife and I take our dogs on a two-mile walk. This daily ritual gives us a chance to talk, breathe in some fresh air, and enjoy the scenery. I don't discuss work-related topics during these walks, but rather I cherish that time together while shedding some calories.

On the weekends I participate in other physical activities, such as playing Pickleball with my wife and friends, along with a visit or two to the gym.

All of these endeavors give my brain a break, enhance my health (I hope), and offer me the opportunity to recharge and relax.

It's obviously up to you how you choose to spend your "free/me" time, but make it a part of your routine and dedicate a block of time to distraction-free fun.

Chapter 10

WHAT'S YOUR LEGACY?

> "I've learned that people will forget what you said, people will forget what you did, but people will never forget how you made them feel."
>
> —*Maya Angelou*

What a beautiful, inspiring and profound quote from Maya Angelou! In a nutshell, that is what a legacy is all about, isn't it? When I read those words, the person who comes to mind for me immediately is my father – John T. Lyons, Jr. – because as incredible as it may seem, I never heard anyone say a bad word about him.

My Dad was the ultimate "glass half full" guy – always there to greet you with a smile, a compliment or with an energetic boost. He befriended everyone he came into contact with and respected all people – regardless of race, title, social status or position. He and my Mom (until her untimely passing at age 54 in 1974) opened up our home graciously and happily to visitors from around the world, and treated them like kings and queens while they were there.

And though he was a master storyteller who kept his audience engaged and delighted, he was also a fantastic listener who always turned the conversation around to ask how the other person was doing. Simply put – he made people feel good about themselves through his gentle, caring and authentic ways.

As a role model and mentor, he was unparalleled. He spread his good cheer not just among his children and family, but everywhere he went, particularly among the disenfranchised or less fortunate. But it was my siblings and me (and our children) who were blessed to receive the largest proportion of his love. He showered us with a never-ending optimism that fueled our self-confidence, helping us become positive contributors to society through his patient tutoring of life lessons.

My father died two months after 9/11, and his funeral was attended by hundreds of people – many of whom I did not recognize. I had an opportunity to speak with some of those I didn't know, and one after another relayed a favorite story, or a kind gesture, or a favor that he did for them that they never forgot. And even though some of them hadn't seen him in years, they went out of their way to come to his funeral to pay their respects. This display of affection was all because of how he "made them feel." He left a beautiful legacy which I envy, but also aspire to.

That is because the older I become and the closer I get to my inevitable departure from this world, the more I think about *my* legacy. What will I be remembered for? What difference have I made? How much positive impact have I had on the people I've come into contact with throughout my life? Will I leave a lasting legacy, like my father, or be a quickly forgotten footnote in our family's history?

As I analyze it, I think quite a bit about how our daily behaviors contribute directly to what our legacy will be. Our morals, ethics, principles and values – and how we live them on a daily basis – form the foundation of how others perceive us. In other words, all those things that constitute our personal brand as discussed in the last chapter. So the question for me (and you) is "How's my brand doing as it relates to creating a lasting legacy?"

I am not afraid of death *per se*, because I have lived a very full, blessed life – but I am redoubling my efforts and scrambling with the time I have left to make up for earlier missed opportunities to be a better person and to make a mark. This has become a sort of preoccupation of mine, and I constantly ask myself the question "What would Dad do?"

WHAT'S YOUR LEGACY?

When I look back, it seems that I have squandered a lot of my life, or wasted opportunities along the way to be more giving and less self-absorbed. And as the sands in the hour glass start to dwindle, I want to speed up my efforts to leave a positive, long-lasting impression – something good, something substantial, and something worthy.

In some ways, that is why I am writing this book. If I can influence even a few people to make positive changes in their lives and to pass on to the next generation suggestions on how to lead a better life, then I won't consider my life to be misspent.

I often wonder how many other people are also thinking about their legacy. Has there been a time where you have asked yourself: "What are people going to remember me for?"

If you are not thinking about it, I encourage you to stop, contemplate it and put it into perspective. Because leaving a strong legacy ultimately ties in to leading a happier life – particularly when you are in service to others.

A legacy can be grounded in teaching or other tangible ways like volunteering your talents and skills, but you can also leave the world a better place simply by being positive, kind, and caring. Every interaction you have with another person has the potential to add to your legacy in a positive manner.

Here are just a few suggestions to build your legacy:

- Volunteer in your community or church with organizations such as the American Red Cross, Big Brothers & Sisters, Homeless Shelters, Make-a-Wish, Salvation Army, *etc.*

- Start a non-profit that will positively impact hundreds (or thousands) of people like Anne Mahlum did with Back on My Feet.

- Plant trees; help out at pet rescue missions; clean up the environment.

- Start a long-term savings plan for your children or grandchildren's college fund.

- Help to build or rebuild a house (perhaps with an organization like Habitat for Humanity).

- Teach reading to inner-city kids.

- Help out in a food kitchen.

There are hundreds of ways to contribute, but whatever it is, it should be something that will leave a lasting impact on others long after you are gone.

Regardless of your age, the time to start working on your legacy is *now*. We often hear stories of people who, on their deathbed, share their regrets about the life they led, and the missed opportunities they never took advantage of during their lives. Here are the five wishes of most dying people:

"I wish I'd had the courage to live a life true to myself, not the life others expected of me."

When people realize that their life is almost over, they lament how many of their daydreams have gone unfulfilled. Most people achieve only some of the things they wanted to accomplish in their lives and die knowing that it was due to choices they had made (or not made) – many times because of the negative influences or pressures from those around them. The message: Be true to yourself.

"I wish I hadn't worked so hard."

This common refrain is heard mostly from older men (who were the main breadwinners in their generation). They missed their children's youth and their partner's companionship because they were at work too much, or on the road. Many men and women deeply regret spending so much of their lives on the treadmill of a work existence. The message: Focus on work–life balance.

"I wish I'd had the courage to express my feelings and chase my dreams."

Due to their life situation and responsibilities (and guilt), some people suppressed their feelings to keep the peace with members of their family and others. As a result, they settled for a mediocre existence and never became who they were truly capable of becoming. The message: You only get one life – go for it!

"I wish I had stayed in touch with my friends."

A lot of individuals do not appreciate or realize the true value and benefits of old friends until their dying weeks when it is too late. Many become so caught up in their lives that they let their golden friendships slip by over the years and they can never recoup those lost opportunities to share happy times and experiences with them. The message: Get in touch with your long-lost friends and family and reconnect. You'll be glad you did.

"I wish I had let myself be happier."

This regret brings us back full-circle to the first chapter in this book and the question "Are You Happy?"

It might be surprising, but this death-bed complaint is fairly common. Many people did not realize until the end that happiness is a choice. They stayed stuck in the "comfort zone" of old patterns and habits. Fear of change had them pretending to others, and to themselves, that they were content. But deep inside, they knew they were unfulfilled.

WHAT'S YOUR LEGACY?

For some it was selecting the wrong life partner or the wrong career path, deciding to not have children (or to have children), among many others. But what a shame that so many people wasted their lives needlessly. The message: Allow yourself to be happy by making better, albeit in some cases, tougher, choices.

Building a legacy also requires doing small day-to-day things on a regular basis. The following are a few examples:

- Spend more time with family in person – not just on the phone, or through texts, email, and Facebook.

- Express more appreciation, love, and respect – in actions and words – to others consistently.

- Take notice of all aspects of your surroundings. Be present. Live in the moment. Stop and smell the roses. Hit the "Pause" button more often, and spend some time alone to reflect and recharge.

- Pay attention to your health – what and how much you eat, and get some exercise three times a week or more.

- Stress less. Every time a worry pops into your head about something that hasn't yet materialized, dwell instead on what is presently going well.

- Follow your passion. So many people I've met are stuck in dead-end jobs. Listen to your gut.

- Try to make a difference every day in someone's life.

In his well-known commencement address at Stanford University in 2005, Apple co-founder Steve Jobs said the following:

"When I was 17, I read a quote that went something like, 'If you live each day as if it were your last, someday you'll most certainly be right.' Since then I have looked in the mirror every morning and asked myself, 'If today were the last day of my life, would I want to do what I am about to do today?' And whenever the answer has been 'no' for too many days in a row, I know I need to change something. Your time is limited… Don't let the noise of others' opinions drown out your own inner voice. And most important, have the courage to follow your heart and intuition… Everything else is secondary."

Well said, Steve. Though you might have been a demanding guy to work for, your legacy is well established, and your name will never be forgotten.

Another person whose legacy touched millions was the beloved Robin Williams. It's hard to find anyone who wasn't moved by this man through his acting and humor, but more importantly through his love, generosity, and authentic spirit. He left us with many valuable life lessons.

Here are ten life lessons we can all learn from Robin Williams – in his words:

1. Do what feeds your creative spirit.

"We don't read and write poetry because it's cute. We read and write poetry because we are members of the human race. And the human race is filled with passion. And medicine, law, business, engineering – these are noble pursuits and necessary to sustain life. But poetry, beauty, romance, love – these are what we stay alive for."

2. Do whatever it takes to make meaningful connections.

"I started performing for my mother, going, 'Love me!' What drives you to perform is the need for that primal connection. When I was little, my mother was funny with me, and I started to be charming and funny for her, and I learned that by being entertaining, you make a connection with another person."

3. Everyone has a story that we know nothing about.

"I think the saddest people always try their hardest to make people happy because they know what it's like to feel worthless, and they don't want anyone else to feel like that."

SET YOURSELF FREE

4. Pursue relentlessly the things you believe.

"No matter what people tell you, words and ideas can change the world."

5. There is a lesson to be found in everything.

"You will have bad times, but they will always wake you up to the stuff you weren't paying attention to."

6. Relationships matter

"I used to think the worst thing in life is to end up all alone. It's not. The worst thing in life is to end up with people who make you feel all alone."

7. Sometimes the best response is no response at all.

"Even fools seem smart when they are quiet."

8. Find the silver lining in every experience.

"Sometimes over things that I did, movies that didn't turn out very well – you go, 'why did you do that?' But in the end, I can't regret them because I met amazing people. There was always something that was worth it."

9. Keep alive the things that make you feel alive.

"You're only given a little spark of madness. You mustn't lose it."

10. Even the most brilliant, confident and most successful people are insecure at times.

"The essential truth is that sometimes you're worried that they'll find out it's a fluke, that you don't really have it. You've lost the muse or – the worst dread – you never had it at all. I went through all that madness early on."

Robin Williams taught us about the importance of self-love and the healing benefits of laughter. The loss of such a great talent and human is still felt today, but his legacy will live on.

In conclusion, I am committed to building a legacy that will have a lasting positive influence on as many people as possible. I aspire to smile more, judge less, and to bring light, joy, and love to my family, friends and those I come into contact with throughout the rest of my life.

Being authentic, sincere and thoughtful will be the guideposts of my roadmap towards creating my legacy – one that I hope I will be proud to leave behind once I check out.

I wish the same for you.

AFTERWORD

Thank you for buying and reading this book. It is my sincere hope that you take to heart some of the suggestions that were offered. Otherwise, it was a waste of your time and money.

Set Yourself Free joins thousands of other "self-help" books, videos, and DVDs that are available in the marketplace. They all have a common theme and message: "If nothing changes, nothing changes."

Albert Einstein's famous definition of insanity is right on: "Doing the same thing over and over again and expecting different results."

The secret sauce in all of this is to **take action now** to pursue your daydreams, whatever they may be. No excuses, no procrastination, no fear. **Start today.** Write out your plan and timetable, follow the simple practices and recommendations contained in this book, and **stick to it.**

Time is marching on, and you will never get it back. You have the power to take fate into your hands and get exactly what you want. **Focus on what will make you happy.** The circle of change ends where it begins.

ABOUT THE AUTHOR

Actor, professional speaker, writer, entrepreneur, hospitality industry executive - Michael Lyons has led a very interesting and diverse life.

His acting career began as a child while living in Paris, France. He appeared in commercials and worked on the film "Paris When It Sizzles," starring Hollywood legends Audrey Hepburn, William Holden and Tony Curtis.

Upon his return to the US, he performed in theatrical plays and musicals in a variety of roles, and also worked on the stage crew of a professional theater in suburban Philadelphia, rubbing shoulders with famous entertainers such as Gordon MacRae, Carol Lawrence, and Chita Rivera.

After graduating from the University of Notre Dame, where he earned a Monogram as a fencer, he went to work in the business world.

In 1990, while working in New York City, he resurrected his dormant acting career, joined SAG (Screen Actors Guild), and began to book commercials, TV roles and other jobs on a regular basis. All the while, he kept his "day job" as a well-respected expert in the travel/meetings industry.

Over the years, Mr. Lyons has worked for 12 different companies in New York City; Stamford and Norwalk, CT; Philadelphia; Columbus, OH; and Minneapolis, and his travels have taken him to most US states, as well as 33 foreign countries.

As an actor, he has amassed dozens of credits in films, TV shows, commercials, and more than 350 live appearances on the home shopping network QVC as a product host. His roles have included speaking parts in the popular Netflix series "House of Cards", "The Sixth Sense," "All My Children," "Veep," "What Would You Do?" "Arrest and Trial," and "Outsiders," among others. He is also an accomplished singer and performs a Frank Sinatra tribute show titled "Mike Sings Frank," featuring classic Sinatra songs from his CD of the same name.

As a motivational speaker, he delivers talks in the US and abroad on how to achieve your goals, pursue your passion, and enhance your personal brand. In addition to this book, he has also authored numerous articles in both travel industry trade journals and consumer magazines and is frequently sought out by the media as one of the experts in the meetings and events industry.

A resident of suburban Philadelphia, he has been married to his lovely wife Lorie since 1974. They are the parents

ABOUT THE AUTHOR

of Mike Jr. (married to Krista), Erin Oosthuizen (married to Simon), and Aimee; and are proud grandparents of seven beautiful children: Ella, Caitlin, Jesse, Ansley, Joshua, Avery and Logan.

CONTACT INFORMATION

For more information and to contact Mike Lyons, please visit:

www.michaeljlyons.com
www.lyonsspeaker.com

LinkedIn: www.linkedin.com/in/mjl810
Email: mike@michaeljlyons.com
Phone: (610)279-9548
Services:

- Keynote Addresses
- Custom On-Site Training Programs/ Workshops
- Corporate Game Show Host
- On-Camera Spokesperson or Interviewer
- Corporate Events or Gala Awards MC
- Panel Discussion Moderator
- Advisory Board Meeting Facilitator
- Actor (Corporate Videos)
- Singer (will customize lyrics for client)
- Consulting Projects

Discount bulk purchases of this book are available.